5|79

£1

Julian Freeman

7. vi. 79

A RADICAL'S GUIDE TO SELF-DESTRUCTION

Books by Angus Black

A New Radical's Guide to Economic Reality

A Radical's Guide to Self-destruction

Angus Black

A Radical's Guide to Self-destruction

HOLT, RINEHART AND WINSTON, INC.
NEW YORK CHICAGO SAN FRANCISCO ATLANTA DALLAS
MONTREAL TORONTO LONDON SYDNEY

Give Pig Capitalists a chance and they'll poison the food you eat, pollute the water you drink, and destroy the air you breath. . . .

Pig Capitalists are raping Mother Nature and you know what that makes them.

CONTENTS

Contents

A RADICAL'S GUIDE TO SELF-DESTRUCTION

1.

GARBAGE TO THE RIGHT OF US,
GARBAGE TO THE LEFT OF US.

New Yorkers, amidst all the usual stink and smell of your city, do you occasionally detect a unique olfactory treat? Well, the wind has to be right for it to happen, but when it does, start breathing through your mouth, for otherwise you'll intake the output of the Staten Island Shit Brigade—fifteen loads a day of 15,000 tons of garbage. Where is it going? To the world's biggest defecatorium, the Staten Island dump.

When Arlo and Co. dumped all of the junk out from Alice and Ray's church, they merely added a wee bit more to what ends up on Staten Island. But that can't go on forever, and it won't, because dumps are filling up. By 1976 NYC will have to look elsewhere to unload its 15,000 tons of crap a day.

Houston decided it didn't like the monotony of the Texas landscape. Its garbage dump is the highest point on the Texas coastal plain and a great drawer of tourists. It can hold no more.

America is literally being inundated by garbage. Every one of you adds almost five pounds of it a day to the pile. That figure is expected to reach seven pounds per day by 2000 A.D. That's progress. During the thirty-five years from 1965 to 2000, we'll have accumulated 10,000,000,000 tons of solid waste. It would cover the entire state of Rhode Island in a twenty-foot layer of various kinds of unneeded items—industrial refuse, junked cars, empty beer cans, used condoms, stems and seeds. The cause of all this garbage is not hard to figure out.

Capitalists produce everything so that it will fall apart. And if it doesn't disintegrate, you'll be convinced that you have to get rid of it because a "new, better" product has just been invented. . . .

"Ladies, have you seen our newest model roller? It can be used for your whole head of hair. That curler you have lying around the house is now as old-fashioned as the bustle."

Capitalists' ever-increasing greed leads them to put their products in fancier and more indestructible containers. Everything you buy has a package over it, and sometimes even the packages are packaged. Have you eaten any good old patriotic American-made cheese lately? The individual slices are neatly (and plastically) cordoned off, lest one of them contaminate its neighbor. Then the plastic wrappers are further wrapped in plastic. Nature can handle a paper bag, but not a plastic one whose half-life is two hundred years. Since people are getting richer, they're buying more and more products, so we see more and more up-and-coming garbage. And since people keep begetting more people, as the Good Book commands them to do, we see even more waste.

Take the example of no-deposit, no-return bottles and cans— seventy-two billion of them each year. They litter our streets, parks, beaches, and also add to the garbage heaps around the country. There was a time when beer and Coke were sold in returnable glass bottles. You paid a nickel at the store, got a nickel when the empty container was returned. At that time a nickel was equivalent to almost forty cents today, so you can imagine that very few bottles were ever left lying around. If you didn't pick them up after a day on the beach, roving bands of kids would do the cleaning up for you.

Bottling firms reused the returned containers—no garbage problem, no litter problem, no excess depletion of our limited resources. Today, we have all three of these problems. Why? Because you prefer not to be bothered with lugging heavy glass bottles back to the corner store. And since competing Capitalists make more money by giving you what you want, they gladly provide no return containers with all beer and Cokes these days. The dumb Capitalist who still used only the more expensive glass bottles would soon find himself bankrupt. Our Capitalist system makes sure that when some-one can get away with doing something cheaper, it will be done cheaper.

3

It's cheaper for both Capitalists and beer drinkers to have someone else, like the Friday morning garbage crew, take care of used no-return bottles and cans. If I throw my empty onto the beach I might never notice it again, if I don't go back there. So why bother? Everybody else, including you, thinks the same way. If I add ten pounds of empties to my garbage pail every week, so what? The city doesn't seem to charge me any more for collecting it. The garbage man never refuses to put it in his truck. He glumly loads in everything that fits and hauls it all to the dump. What happens then? Basically the same thing that happened during the Roman Empire. The land is filled in with some of the garbage; the rest is burned. Those landfills are breeding grounds for rats and disease. Garbage incinerators add to air pollution, because over 70 percent of the city incinerators have no pollution control whatsoever. The Federal Environmental Control Administration declared the nation's dumps and incinerators a "national disgrace."

But something has to be done, otherwise we'll end up all garbage and little else. There have been numerous stopgap measures. Philadelphia still depends on a daily band of pig farmers who truck swill back to their Jersey farms. Czechago installed the nation's biggest incinerator, an oven that eats up sixteen thousands tons of Daley's refuse each day. Milwaukee and Denver are looking for places in the sticks they can ship their waste to. And more bays are being filled.

Filling wasn't a bad idea—at first. Some of New York's most valuable land was originally water. If you visited either of its two world fairs, you may not have known it but you were stepping on millions of tons of crushed cars and mutilated refrigerators.

Some cities in the Midwest are making trash heaps into

skiable resort areas. Almost anything's an improvement there, as anyone who's had the misfortune of living in the middle of middle America will readily admit.

There have been other schemes. Some bright Texas engineer at one time thought up a modern-day conversion of straw into gold by making garbage into fertilizer and heaping it onto compost piles. One trouble, no one wanted to buy the resultant super manure, as L.A. soon found out when it tried to sell the stuff. Since that particular kind of compost pile stinks like gangrenous intestines, Houston had to close its pile down.

Another possibility is compacting garbage into little squares. One company can compress five thousand pounds of trash into four cubic feet. This just forestalls the time when garbage overtakes us. And besides, who's going to take all those four-foot cubes from the big city where they're made?

All these solutions are merely temporary. Is there anything real that can be done for the future? Maybe. One possibility is recycling. That is, junk could be reused so as to minimize the amount of material really wasted. Some companies are already doing this. Reynolds Metal Company is offering $200 per ton for discarded aluminum in L.A. and Miami. They're only doing so because it's now profitable to recycle this metal. We can't ever rely on the good grace of Capitalists to solve our problems. As long as they can push off the cost of garbage on others they will.

But of course so will everyone else. The only way to get people to stop using and discarding cans and no-returns is to impose costs on them. Bowie, Maryland, started fining those who sell nonreturnables at the rate of $100 per day, as of April 1, 1971. Better yet, since it is well recognized that empties impose costs on society in the form of littered landscapes and mounting garbage piles, a tax could be imposed on them. The proceeds of the tax would cover all cleanup and disposition costs. People turning in empties would be given a portion of the tax proceeds. This tax would have to be applied everywhere, otherwise some sneaky bastards would buy beer and Coke in those places where the tax wasn't applied and return the empties to places where there was a reward.

A British scientist, Dr. N.A. Iliff, suggested that the solution to littering with empties could be solved by "the cultivation of better manners." Now there's a typical half-assed comment by someone totally unaware of economic reality. We'll get nowhere by depending on everyone else's goodwill and you know that, even though your philanthropical soul hates to admit it. Even if some people don't leave empties in the parks, enough do so as to wreck the environment. *Everyone* must be faced with the true cost of his actions if we are to solve the garbage problem. That's why a tax on containers is needed. I venture that the rate which will really cover all the costs involved with nonreusable, nonbiodegradable containers will be so high that Capitalists will end up switching back to reusable bottles—no more litter and less use of limited natural resources, since fewer containers need be made.

But that won't solve the rest of the garbage crisis, for we'll still be throwing out as much other stuff as before, like seven million junked cars a year, several million tons of discarded plastic packaging, and a hundred million used toothbrushes. I really don't understand the situation. The garbage piles are growing bigger, yet I only have to pay a few dollars a month for the city to relieve me of anything I can carry to the street every Friday morning. Why will I stop creating so much garbage if there's no incentive for me to do so? And how about you? As Yossarian said, "If everyone's doing it, you'd be a fool not to."

How responsive will you be to a campaign against "excessive" use of plastics? When there are plastic bags on a roll above the vegetables and paper bags below the counter, which do and will you choose when grocery shopping? And what about all those things you buy in fancy plastic containers? You say you don't have a choice these days. Well, if that's really true it's because you're getting what you asked for. Since people selling things try to provide their customers with what they want, you must have shown that you like pretty plastic packages. Otherwise greedy Capitalists would be offering something less fancy and more biodegradable.

The solution to too much garbage is to make private citizens, Capitalists, and even our benevolent government pay a higher price to get rid of their garbage. The results will depend on how high the price is. In fact, if each city raises its fee for garbage collection to say $100 per 55-gallon canfull, I'll bet not too many people will use plastic bags for their vegetables when they go to the grocery. I'll bet you'll refuse bags for every little thing you buy. I'll bet that companies will come up with products that last longer, because you'll want to buy only that kind, in order to avoid paying such high disposal costs.

Capitalists will think twice about unloading all their industrial by-products at the city dump. Recycling will then be more profitable.

What? You don't like the idea of having to pay so much to get rid of your garbage? We have sent men to the moon, so we could send garbage, but I think you realize that that might cost you a little more than my solution.

2.

FOR SALE--COW'S TEETH

There's a place in these United States where the grass is blue. Not Kentucky but Steubenville, Ohio. In fact the grass is iridescent blue. The cows eat it and their teeth fall out. Though nobody knows what's specifically wrong with the grass, there is no doubt about the cause—our old friend, industrial pollution. The lucky people in Steubenville gained international renown when a federal agency discovered that they were living in the grimiest town in the country. A mere $50\frac{1}{2}$ tons of pollutants are dropped on every square mile every year. Some lucky people get an average of 127 tons. Compare those figures with the federally recommended "livable" standard of 15 tons; that's enough to make you feel pretty lousy.

But living in a quiet Ohio River mill town isn't so bad. Houses only have to be repainted yearly, and some people get to do it even more often; one night a good rain brought down so much hydrogen sulphide that several hundred houses turned pitch black. Women get to wash their hair three times a week.

Why is Steubenville such a paradise on earth? Because the National Steel Corp., Wheeling-Pittsburg Steel Corp., and about one hundred other Capitalist firms have plants in the area. And why shouldn't they? The Ohio River is a great place to dump garbage, and so far no one in the vicinity has done much to stop the pollution of the air. Old-timers in Steubenville say that the situation has improved. They can recollect when old-fashioned open-topped steel furnaces were used, and street lights in the city had to be left burning twenty-four hours a day.

Did steel Piggies change to cleaner furnaces because they cared about all the pollution they were causing? No way. They changed because it was cheaper to use the newer type of equipment; the companies could make more profit that way. Why should the Piggies worry about pollution? If one Capitalist decided to keep the air and water clean around his plant he'd end up spending lots of bread buying pollution control gadgets. His costs would rise while those of his competitors stayed the same. He'd end up making less in profits. He might even go out of business. And why? Because of you, dear consumer. Do you care how your products are made and how much pollution is involved in the process? All you want is the most for the least. That's how you get your joy in life, otherwise you wouldn't be working at the best-paying job you could find. You work to get income. With the income you buy things that you obviously get satisfaction from. If you get something you want cheap, that leaves you more income to buy other things. Capitalists make the most money by selling you what you want at the lowest price possible. You may not agree, but the fact still remains.

Now it's true that Capitalists screw each other when given half a chance. You've got to remember that the very nature of the pig is greed; the thing that puts the oink in the pig is his greed. If he can get away with having others pay for part of what he's producing, he'll do it, because then he can sell his products cheaper. You end up rewarding him for this by buying more at the cheaper price.

Look at a steel mill. The cost of making steel includes what's spent for ore, machinery, furnace tenders, bookkeepers, managers, executives, and so on. But all those by-products belched out of the steel mills' smokestacks and vomited from their drainage pipes cost society something too.

When the smoke in the air makes the workers feel as if they had been living on a steady diet of rancid MacDonald burgers, the steel mill ends up having to pay them higher wages, because some cats won't accept low wages when they know that there's a chance of getting lung cancer from working in a polluted plant. Some, however, may take that risk if paid high salaries. Besides, there will be Pig Capitalists elsewhere whose factories don't have so much pollution hanging in the air. These smart dudes will bid away some steel mill workers by merely offering safer working conditions.

But steel mill owners don't have to pay for the vomit they pour into adjacent rivers, lakes, and oceans, or the crap they blow into the air which travels to other places. Pig Capitalists treat the air and water as if it were free for them to destroy. And it *is* free, to them. Water and certainly air are usually owned by no one—they are common property.

In the case of bodies of water the state may own them, but it does not force polluters to pay for the muck that is poured into them. The true cost to society of a piece of steel includes all the costs imposed by the pollution the steel mill causes. Who pays for it? You and I, brothers and sisters, because we're the ones who suffer from smelly air, lung cancer, emphysema, fouled lakes, rivers, oceans. But if we use steel products we also get the benefit of lower prices. So it's really a matter of some people getting a good deal while others suffer.

How should we make the mothers stop polluting? One way is to haul them into court, and that's what some groups have been doing. Notice that it's usually a *group* of people who sue, because pollution seldom affects only one person. If it did, the person affected and the polluter would find it advantageous to contract an agreement which would clear things up, assuming of course that our courts made the contract enforceable.

Groups of conservationists have started pressing suits because pollution damages natural beauty. Two Phoenix, Arizona, professors sued six Piggie copper producers for $2 billion because of all the damage to the "natural beauty of the environment" caused by their smelters. The suit also mentioned that the health of the area's inhabitants had been seriously damaged.

One stooge lawyer who works for U.S. Steel, Sun Oil, and Monsanto Chemical remarked that "the amount of [pollution] litigation over the country is staggering." Big companies are spending years in the courtroom arguing with antipollution suitors. But, we do have laws on the books against almost all forms of pollution, so why all this legal hassle? Well, for one thing, many of those laws were drawn up a hundred years ago, so the fines aren't very big relative to what Piggies are making today. Capitalists have discovered that it's a lot cheaper to pay the assessed fine and go on polluting. In addition, most antipollution laws aren't enforced because city officials don't want to shake up the local Capitalists. After all, those stinking steel mills provide jobs and tax dollars.

One place did, however, have the guts to fight it out with the Piggies. Olin Corp., Virginia, had been making soda ash and other chemicals since 1895. It's also been dumping poisonous effluent into the Holston River since 1895. The state's Water Control Board finally decided to crack down. They raised purity standards for plant waste outflow into the river. The Piggies at the Olin Plant decided that the standard "proved impossible to meet" so the decision was to close the plant and put six hundred employees out of work. "Impossible to meet"? Pure crap! The Olin Piggies really meant that it would cost them "too" much money to install the necessary equipment to clean things up.

Since those profit-hungry bastards are out to make the most bread possible, they decided it would be better to close the plant down and either produce something else or build a plant where they wouldn't have such "impossible" controls layed on them. Our Capitalist system (with your aid and abettal) makes sure that Piggies will screw the public whenever they can. When the Virginia Water Control Board stopped Olin Corp., the Corporation's officers just looked somewhere else for a chance to produce without paying for pollution control equipment. The result—lost jobs in Virginia; but as the enforcement director for the Control Board said, ". . . in a choice between employment and a clean river, we prefer to have a clean river."

The moral of this story is that even though Capitalists are

polluting, most places where it is happening allow it to continue because jobs are at stake. No one's forcing those of you who work in the steel mills of Gary or Steubenville to stay there, right? No one who worked for Olin in Virginia quit because he knew the company was ruining the Holston River. And nobody stops buying products from U.S. Steel just because that firm is destroying the environment. Let's face it. Every one of you tries to maximize your own happiness. When given the chance, you'll let the ecology be destroyed if you're individually better off.

Now for another example of how laws make Piggies turn around and screw things up elsewhere, let's look at West Virginia. A new coal mine safety law went into effect there. The cost seemed "impossible" to coal Capitalists, so they're now strip mining all over the countryside, destroying the ecology right and left. It's almost as if you've got to stop them from producing anything in order to save the environment. And in a very strict sense, that's true. All production involves some destruction.

Even if we pass more stringent laws against pollution, we still have a problem nabbing the polluters. Right now the U.S. is faced with a conspiracy of unheard-of proportions. It's the Fly-Ash-by-Night Conspiracy. In cities where strict antipollution laws have been passed, the graveyard shift is dumping all the previous day's waste into the air and water. How do we know about these nefarious nighttime activities? For one, in New York City, apartment residents often wake up with a hefty serving of soot on their window sills, all accumulated during the night. In Pittsburgh, we know the polluting is always done in the early morning because in the suburbs people find their cars covered with ash when they wake up, even if they had just washed them the night before. Watchmen on the railroad bridge spanning the Buffalo River say that they watch an eery spectacle every night.

They see a parade of seething effluents pass by, covering the river from bank to bank. But they don't mind because it breaks up the monotony, adds a little color to their jobs. (Pollution is not bad for everyone, you know.)

So even with laws against pollution, there still remains the problem of detection. To overcome this, society must be willing to bear the added price of policing the Capitalist polluters. That means you've got to be willing to have less of what you now buy in order to have a cleaner environment. (A lot of you when faced with the choice would say "To hell with the environment.")

But aren't there ways of stopping industrial filth that won't cost society such a wad? Why don't we force companies to recycle all their waste products? First of all, you can be sure that the profit maniacs who run all the corporations in the U.S. aren't going to do anything unless it pays them to. Asking a Piggie to please recycle his effluents will get you the same response you'll have by asking all your friends to buy only from ecology-conscious manufacturers. Capitalists recycle when they can make more bread by doing so; otherwise they happily continue to muck up the environment. So far most resources aren't scarce enough nor laws against pollution effective enough to induce Piggies to use recycled waste products. One unlucky Capitalist in Houston is finding out this sad reality the hard way. He started Metropolitan Waste Conversion Corp. The plant separates waste into paper, metal, crushed glass, and garden composts. Each week he ends up with 1200 tons of good solid paper, but only sells 200. Why? Because at the price he sells it, it doesn't pay many people to substitute his used paper for new paper. The same story is true for all the recycled products this little Piggy takes to market. The business of recycling has cost the guy $2,000,000 during three years of operation. How many Capitalists will do that just to save our environment?

When laws are enforced, Piggies come up with schemes that still enable them to come out on top. Olin closed down; other companies find other solutions. Masonite was dropping effluents into one Southern river for years, until one day a large number of fish died. Unfortunately for Masonite, the governor of the state just happened to have a mansion overlooking the river. The sight of hundreds of thousands of dead fish floating by his glass picture window while he sipped mint juleps brought immediate response: Stop the effluents or close down the plant! Faced with such a choice Masonite found that they could recycle their effluents. The stuff is now processed into animal feed. Never underestimate the smarts of Capitalist technology when something's threatening their ability to make as much bread as they're used to. Since you like as much of everything as possible, they try as much as possible to sell it to you.

You have to be careful, though, when making a law that restricts only one form of pollution. Some foreigner named Lavoisier once came up with the law of conservation of mass, and so it is. You can only change the form of pollution, but the total amount of crap is constant. Take, for example, a paper pulp mill. Force it to stop dumping in the rivers and it might find that the cheapest alternative is to pile the waste on the banks of the river; then we're faced with a garbage and smell problem. Make a company put soot-reducing precipitators on its smokestacks and they'll drop all the accumulated ash in a nearby dump, again adding to the garbage crisis.

The solution to the problem is obviously to make polluters pay for *all* the economic costs of their pollution, no matter what form it takes. I propose that the simplest way is to tax the profits out of them. Tax the water polluters in proportion to the value of the economic losses that the crap they dump into rivers and lakes causes us. Tax air polluters in proportion to the costs to us from all the soot they spew into the air. Tax freshness polluters in proportion to how smelly they make the air. Use the tax proceeds for environmental cleanup. The tax shouldn't be the same everywhere in the country, because some places can handle some pollution without ill effects. A stream can cleanse itself if not too much junk is put in it. A smelly factory out in the Arizona desert probably won't bother anybody except the people working in it, nor will the soot from a plant located two hundred miles equidistant from nowhere.

One thing that must be remembered: Our pollution laws and taxes should not be based on a first-come, first-serve principle. If you live in a nice clean neighborhood and a Capitalist decides to move next to you with a smelly factory, you cry bloody murder. But what if the factory were there first? Would you feel as justified in getting the factory to be clean smelling? Probably not. But a correct economic solution should treat both cases the same. It really shouldn't matter who came first. That means both parties in *all* cases should bear part of the cost of the offending action. You'd probably commit me if you could because I'm telling you that you should pay for clean air and clean water. But you should; otherwise control of pollution would be based purely on who was to get there first, you or a factory. All this just means that a tax on pollution shouldn't by itself be so large as to stop *all* pollution.

But remember that in order to tax you have to be able to assess the amount of pollution a Capitalist is producing. That means we're going to have to be willing to pay the price of detection and measurement of environmental destruction. That won't be small change either.

Once the taxes are put into effect, everyone, except the Piggies who have to pay, will be happy, right? Well, not quite. The nature of the Capitalist beast is to always try to screw everyone else. Tax him a little and he starts making less money than before. That hurts. Piggies who use the most pollution-producing production methods are going to find their profits slipping away, because they'll be taxed the most. What'll they do? Some will take their capital some place else where they can at least make what they consider to be a normal rate of return on their dollars invested.

Others will spend money to invent methods of manufacturing that produce less pollution. And still others will just pay the tax. That means there'll be some pollution around, but I don't mind, since I know that elimination of every bit of it would result in a pretty grim, expensive existence for those of us who like to do more than contemplate our navels out in the country. All of these events will mean just one thing to you and me—Piggies are going to charge us more money for their products. All the goods formerly made in big stinky factories will cost more. Why? Because some Capitalists who own those factories will be taxed so much they'll go into other businesses, thus reducing available supplies. Other Piggies will pay the tax or install costly antipollution devices and end up passing these costs to you and me. Since the pollution tax will apply to all who produce, all Piggies in pollution-producing industries will have to pay it, and they'll all raise their prices. The market will necessarily be smaller since not all consumers will buy as much in goods as before because of the new higher prices.

When Capitalists are forced to pay for pollution, they make sure that you pay too, because you're responsible for their polluting in the first place. If you didn't want to buy products at the lowest possible price, then Capitalists might have installed antipollution equipment years ago and just charged you more.

As Karl Marx once said: You should pay for what you get.

3.

THE RAPE OF THE WILD

The U.S. used to be covered with hundreds of millions of acres of trees—pure, beautiful wilderness. Then along came Paul Bunyan and Babe the Blue Ox. Chop, chop, chop. And when there was nothing left to cut, on to another part of the country. If you've ever seen a stretch of logged wilderness you know what I'm talking about. Why spend money on special defoliants in Vietnam? Just send over a few timber Capitalists; there won't be a tree left standing.

The fight to save our natural wilderness isn't new. Large-scale conservation efforts started in T. Roosevelt's time, with Gifford Pinchot at the head of the ship. Since then, courageous conservationists have been able to prevent the rape of the wilds from getting out of hand. Today the Sierra Club leads the battle against the profit-hungry tree cutters.

Why do the Piggies want to cut so many trees in the first place? Obviously because cut trees can be further cut up into lumber, which can then be used for houses, furniture, and billy clubs for federal marshalls, state police, and other various and sundry types of Pig.

If lots of timber is cut, that means lots of lumber will be around. And in order to sell all of it, Capitalists will have to lower prices. That means houses will be cheaper. That means poor people can live better. If we conserve trees, the reverse will be true. I guess we're forced to conclude that conservation isn't necessarily beneficial for everyone. Capitalists can't make as much profit if we don't let them rape our forests, but who cares about Capitalists anyway? If you screw them though, you will also get screwed with higher housing costs, whether you own or rent.

You might think that's just a very small price to pay for wilderness, which *everybody* benefits from. Aside from the fact that some parts of the forest get so raunchy that they become breeding grounds for insects and therefore should be cut, I must agree that lots of people get to see the wilderness, to hunt and to fish, and to backpack too. And they derive immense pleasure from this trip. But who are these people? How many Blacks from the Ghetto go backpacking? How many low-income whites take to the hills with little more than some special, freeze-dried, dehydrated, nutrients-added food and a down-filled, hand-sewn, superlight-weight mummy bag on their backs? You know what? It's usually upper-class snobs who benefit from wilderness areas.

And you know what else? The Sierra Club is filled to the brim with upper-class, upper-income, snobby intellectuals. Many studies have shown it. One was even entitled "Conservation: An Upper-middle Class Social Movement." The study revealed that the dudes in the Sierra Club and other conservationist groups were all people who were well-educated and from high-income occupations. 82 percent had college or graduate education. 75 percent were considered to be in high-status occupations, such as medicine, law, and college teaching.

When the Sierra Club asks that the wilderness be saved, it means saved for rich Sierra Club members and screw the rest of the public who are too poor to ever get away for a week of backpacking.

What do the Sierra Club and the Wilderness Society mean when they support conservation anyway? Should we "conserve" all our trees, all our coal, all our oil, all our natural gas? During the nineteenth century many people didn't think we should conserve anything. For example, the U.S. commissioner of patents thought that "it is preposterous to suppose the supplies of coal can ever be exhausted or even become scarce."

Now there's an asinine comment. Since the store of coal is fixed, we have to run out of it someday if we just keep burning it. But does that mean we shouldn't use coal, or oil, or any other natural resource? And what about things that replace themselves, like trees? How many should be cut?

To answer these questions we must first realize that whenever you do something, there is a cost involved. If you don't use coal to generate electricity, you've got to use something else, or not generate as much electricity. We can't have everything, because there's a limit to how much Mother provides us. Now our friend Gifford Pinchot said that "conservation means the greatest good for the greatest numbers, and that for the longest time." But that's impossible. If one group of people gets something, another group doesn't. And how can we get all that "good . . . for the longest time" with conservation? Conservation means conserve, not use. How do we get any good *now* from coal if we leave it in the ground? Pinchot must have been thinking of Nirvana when he made his statement. If we were to use our resources for "the longest time" we'd never use them at all! No roach clips, no electronic vibrating dildoes, nothing.

Conservation can't mean that. It really involves using just the right amount of our resources at just the right time. We want to get the most good out of what's available on this earth. How do we know what is the most? Easy, just look at the benefits for different rates of resource use. One rate is zero for now and ever after. The other is everything now, nothing later. And in between there are any number of other possibilities. We are conserving our natural resources if we use them at rates which yield the most benefit for society. And to be sure, the same size benefit available a hundred years from now doesn't count as much to us as it would if it were available today. Screwing future generations? Not at all. They'll be better off from the greater wealth we'll leave them. After all, income is just the amount of wealth we can enjoy today. The larger our wealth, the more income we have and the more things we can enjoy.

Look at iron ore. We can dig it up today to make a steel building which adds to our wealth and to that of future generations. We and they derive utility from it. That same iron ore could be left in the ground to be dug up a hundred years from now and made into something then, but a hundred years of no measurable utility would have been piled up. Future generations would have inherited iron ore instead of a steel building. They might be better off, but only unless there's something fantastically valuable for them to make the iron ore into. And for sure, all generations in the interim would probably be worse off.

Anyway, the decision about how much ore to leave for future generations has to be made *today,* right? Our grandkids aren't around yet to tell us what they want, so we've got to use our best judgment. Who's us? Uncle Sam? For the love of Jesus X. Christ, no. Ask our government to plan for the future and we'll end up supporting a nation of sinecured bureaucrats, all living in Washington, D.C., the octopus of world fascism. I hate to say it, but Capitalists are the best ones to make the decision. They're out for the most profits possible. They'll make sure that they get the right amount of information about what you want today and all the potential uses and value of our resources for all future periods. That way they can make the most money.

But what happens when we run out of resources, you ask. Man's history is one of never-ending success in discovering new resources to replace old. Besides, the scarcer a resource becomes, the more expensive it gets. People start looking elsewhere for a substitute long before the stuff is gone.

You must also realize that when we conserve one resource we use another, so we can't conserve *all* our resources.

"Conservation" usually refers to a specific resource, such as trees or fish or Bald Eagles. But even then it's not clear what we should do for conservation because so many things are interrelated. Take the protection bestowed on both salmon and seals in the Pacific Northwest. Both are legally protected from rapacious fishermen, but not from each other. Seals are salmon freaks. So the conservation of both creatures really benefits mainly the seals.

Some conservationists think they're doing the world a favor by supporting the use of natural resources so that the yearly take is as large as it can be without endangering the resource's future. That's pure bull. It takes men, machines, materials, and time to pull, for example, fish from the sea. Pulling out "maximum sustainable yields" may end up costing more than it's worth to get that many fish out of the ocean every year.

But I still haven't explained the rape of the woods, which all of us can see with our eyes. The woods were raped by Piggies because it didn't cost them anything to ruin a forest. Typically they didn't own the land then, so they just cut down all the worthwhile trees and went on to other virgin territories. It didn't pay in the eighteenth and nineteenth centuries to conserve any trees, except the rotting and hard-to-reach ones. If some conservationist timberman (did they exist?) decided it wasn't a good idea to cut down all the worthwhile trees, he'd eventually go out of business. Why? Because our profit system rewards low-cost sellers. Any Capitalist conserving trees would end up with higher costs, because he'd have to move more often than his fellow Piggies who were cutting all over the place without regard to the effects on the forests. And would you buy lumber which was more expensive but harvested by a conservationist? If you say yes, you're an unmitigated liar.

The rape of the woods happened because so much timberland

was free, that is, common property. Nobody owned it, so it didn't pay anyone to take care of it.

It's just like what happened back then to a juicy innocent fifteen-year-old thrown out in the cold cruel world alone, with no father, brothers, old man, or Women's Lib to protect her "rights." She was left to the mercy of drooling wolves who didn't care about conserving anything for the future. How much attention do you think they paid to any ill effects on her forests? She was all used up in no time.

If we were to sell all the tree land to Piggies, do you think they'd cut it all down? Christ no, because they're looking at profit not just for today but for many years to come. It pays them to cut down trees only if the use-value of lumber is higher today than it will be, say, fifty years from now. Of course, the value today to the Piggies of, say, $100 they might receive for a cut tree is certainly not the same $100 in fifty years. It's less. Say you owed some cat $100, and you told him, okay, man, I'll lay it on you in fifty years. He'd be an ass to accept the deal. You could stash much less than $100 in a savings account today and still be able to pay him back the $100 in fifty years. Why? Simply because of all the interest you'd have earned in the meantime.

Selling all the trees to Capitalists seems like a surefire disaster for campers. There'd be no campsites left! But if we think that way, then we're really saying that campsites have no value to campers. If campers really want to camp, they'll be willing to pay for it. After all, that's the only true test of how much somebody wants something. If he *really* wants it, he'll give up something else to get it. And apparently campers are willing to pay for the pleasure of camping even now when we have "free" or very low entry fee public forest areas. In 1969 there were 657,000 private campgrounds available to outdoor buffs. That was a 15 percent increase over the number in 1968.

Anyway, free camping areas aren't free at all, that is, not to society as a whole. These forests cost something every second of every day of every year. What do they cost? The value of those services they would be giving to other people in another form, like lumber for an unheated outhouse, like a commune's private homestead, or like munched up into paper for books like the one you're reading. (I use the term loosely.) And when you think about it a little more you realize that the real cost of a free camping area is the value of that land in its best alternative use, that is, the use that would pay the most. That use might be houses for the poor.

If the rich Sierra Club bloods want to save wilderness areas, why shouldn't these cats who use those "saved" areas pay the true cost of them? Why don't they buy up the land with their own bread? But if they succeed in getting the government to "save" an area so that they can take their kids backpacking, then why shouldn't the government make those rich bastards pay a user charge? The government could then take the proceeds to compensate all of those who are getting screwed because of, for example, higher housing costs due to less lumber being supplied by loggers.

Power to the People, not to the few wealthy intellectuals who like peace, quiet, and wilderness. Like, they can pay for it if they really want it.

4.

FROM SEA TO SHINING SEA

Pig Capitalists have destroyed our air, destroyed our forests, destroyed our lakes and streams, and now they're destroying man's last great resource—the oceans. No one needs to be reminded of the thousands of dead birds, the blackened beaches, and stinky air after the Santa Barbara oil blowout. Or after the Torrey Canyon disaster. Or after all the spills in the Gulf of Mexico.

And few are unaware that Capitalists are overfishing our seas. Old-timers can still recollect when they could catch albacore and barracuda off the pier at Santa Monica.

Now the days of shining seas are gone. But need they be gone forever? Can't we stop the Piggies from cheating all of us out of our last great natural resource? Why are there all these problems anyway?

Well, take a good look at commercial ocean fishing. Nobody owns the high seas (and not even the low). People like to eat fish, especially if it's cheaper than other foods. People have to eat something, so Capitalists take to the seas—and not just a few, but hundreds of thousands throughout the world. Every boat owner tries to make as much bread as possible. If you let him, he'll fish the shit out of any stretch of water. Why should he care about the long-run consequences of all boat owners acting just the way he does? If he slows down on the take, some other greedy bastard will just be able to get more fish, and more money. Our profit system makes sure that every fishing boat will take in as many fish as it profitably can.

And our profit system is based on all your desires. Since you realize that every dollar you spend on food means one less dollar you can spend on other things, you naturally spend as little as possible to satisfy your particular level of food consumption, both in quantity and quality. Let's say one particular fisherman didn't want to "overfish." He'd only make a relatively small catch. To make a living he'd feel he would have to charge a higher price for his fish. Would his story about not wanting to overfish induce you to pay him a higher price than you'd have to pay the greedy fisherman next to him selling his huge catch for a lower price? No. All you care about is your own welfare. How can you imagine what overfishing means anyway until it affects you individually later on?

And nobody out there on the water cares about overfishing. Since no one boat owner has any say over how the ocean is used, there's no one who has any individual incentive to reduce his intake of slippery protein. Therein lies the real problem.

The ocean is free to all comers. It's a big piece of common property. No one has exclusive rights over most of the oceans. Just as with the rape of the forests, Capitalists end up harvesting too many fish. They do it to satisfy your greed for low-cost food. What's more, there are too many small inefficient fishing boats. For example, it has been estimated that 75 to 82 percent of the fishing boats in one Alaskan region were economically unnecessary from 1955 to 1959. Today even more boats are wasteful. The estimate for the Puget Sound is 50 percent. And since commercial fishing uses resources that therefore can't be used for anything else, the cost to society of all this overfishing is $50,000,000 a year just for Pacific commercial salmon alone.

The overfishing of our oceans has become so obvious in some places that states have felt the necessity of imposing limits and of regulating legal fishing seasons. This is one possible solution. But it won't work forever, because our government doesn't lay claim to all the ocean waters, although it talks as if it owned them. Fishing Capitalists are still able to overfish unregulated areas, thus threatening the survival of many species. Witness the Russian superfisher—an immense mother (ship) with all the equipment to detect, clean, and preserve millions upon millions of fish, along with a fleet of little bastard offspring boats that do all the actual catching. Quite a racket! Does it tick you off to hear about our fishermen being put in jail in Peru because of a violation of that country's two-hundred-mile limit? It did me, at first. What right do the Peruvians have to all that ocean space? But that's ultimately the only solution possible. Every square foot of ocean has to be transformed from common property into some sort of exclusive property—owned and regulated by governments or by individuals.

If a Pig Capitalist exclusively owned all the salmon ocean space, would he overfish it? No, because then he wouldn't be making as much bread as possible. What our government should do, and every other government too, is stake out a claim to all the various parts of the ocean. Then the idea would be to sell or lease fishing rights for individual parcels of the oceans. The rights for each individual parcel could only be sold to one Capitalist, though, otherwise we'd get overfishing again. And the right would be sold to the highest bidder. Competition among Capitalists would result in the state getting a "good" price and reaping most of the profit. The Capitalists who succeeded in getting fishing rights to a parcel would still make enough money to have the investment pay off.

And this scheme isn't impossible now, although it would have been a hundred years ago. Today we have relatively cheap electronic detection equipment that would allow the owner of the fishing rights to prevent others from using his parcel of ocean for fishing on the sly. Of course, he would probably sell partial rights to fishermen to do the "correct" amount of fishing; that is, he wouldn't allow overfishing because it would be cutting into his own wallet. This might cause some problems for a cat rowing from Boston to England in a ten-foot dinghy. Imagine all the customs inspections he would have to go through.

Unfair to Indian and Eskimo fishermen? You bet your sweet

ass, but since the government would be getting the maximum revenue possible from the oceans, it could very easily give the poor native fishermen more than they are now making when every dude on the coast, poor and rich, can and is overfishing.

I still haven't said anything about all the accidental oil spills and the deliberate flushing of sludge and debris from oil tankers into our oceans. That black magic is nonbiodegradable; it just sits there in the water minding its own business. At the rate we're going, the seas will soon be shining even without a full moon.

Do you think a Pig Capitalist would act differently? That's like thinking that if you shoot up with Meth you'll immediately crash. Since up until recently nobody even bothered to make Standard Oil, Philips, and the rest of the pack shell out for any damage their oil caused to users of the oceans, it didn't pay them to be as careful as some of us would have liked. You're probably better off *because* of the carelessness of oil companies. Their carelessness means they spend less getting oil to the U.S. That ultimately means cheaper gas for your car. You don't seem to mind that, do you? And if you never go near the ocean, I'll bet you never really want oil companies to spend any money preventing oil spills, right? Therefore, those of you reaping the benefits of low-priced gas are being subsidized by everyone who enjoys clean beaches and pure ocean waters.

We've got to do something. We've got to get each coastal state to impose totally unlimited damage liability for all who foul its waters. The state has to act as if it were a Pig Capitalist itself and actually owned the common property called ocean. Hit the oil bastards where it hurts. When the Piggies know they'll have to pay for all the animal life destroyed, all the recreation curtailed, and all the discomfort to everyone affected by any oil spills or blowouts, then they'll take the right safeguards against any accidents. Why? Because it will be cheaper for them in the long run.

After all, profit makers are, by definition, out for profit, because that's where their heads are at. The only reason that's so is because you seem to like to have the best life possible, even if you vaguely realize that somebody else is footing part of the bill.

5.

NOISE POLLUTION CAN'T KILL
(IT CAN ONLY BLOW YOUR MIND
--FOR GOOD)

      Caesar didn't get off too well with noisy chariots tooling around the streets, so he banned chariot driving at night. Modern-day chariots aren't banned though, night or day, so we find the noise level during the rush hours almost unbearable. Noise in New York City reaches 95 decibels at 5 P.M. Since prolonged exposure to only 85 decibels of noise causes ear damage, it's no wonder that the traffic storm troopers are always yelling—they can't even hear themselves.

Noise is all over: sirens, horns, jackhammers, air compressors, motorcycles, garbage trucks, jets, helicopters, power boats, screaming rape victims, and rock bands.

The noise level in society may be bad now, but it's bound to get worse. A government study found that the din is doubling every decade. The old Chinese noise torture may be experienced by all of us in the future, merely by stepping out on a congested city street.

The effects of noise on our ears are obvious. The effect on our heads is less so. Since the level of this form of pollution has been gradually rising, we haven't noticed how it's affected our psyches and general health. Doctors now maintain that noise contributes to heart disease. Excessive sound speeds up the heart, constricts the arteries, and dilates the pupils. Constant noise may also lead to stomach ulcers, enuresis (pissing too much), and impaired sight.

It also blows your mind. The French maintain that in addition to causing impotency in rats, excessive sound creates anxiety neurosis. Their study results claim that 70 percent of neurosis in Parisians is caused by noise. Since prolonged noise makes rats turn gay and eat their offspring, it's not surprising that frogs don't relate to it too well. French dudes got so uptight about unwanted sound that they ripped off some of their own people. (Emotional bastards, *n'est-ce pas?*) And one Black cat in the Bronx offed one of the four little kids playing underneath his apartment. What do you expect? He worked nights; those kids yelling and shouting were keeping him from his sleep.

What's the cause of all this unwanted sound? Although much of it comes from Capitalists as they devour our natural resources to make us houses, streets, and cars, a lot is caused by you.

When you blow your car horn, Little Boy Blue, no one is forcing you to do it. But you force unwanted noise on everyone around you. So do all other horn freaks. Individually, people can't stop you or all the other thousands of drivers, but if enough people are really ticked off, laws can be passed and big fines slapped on offending blowers. The "quietest city in the U.S.," Memphis, Tennessee, has effectively banned most horn-blowing all the time. (Does that account for the Memphis Sound?)

Unfortunately, there's no other way out of the hornblowing dilemma, except perhaps imposing a user charge. Meters could be installed in all cars. They would register the total number of blows a year. During annual automobile inspections, the number on a car meter would be recorded and each car owner would be assessed a blow fee proportional to how many times he used his horn. (Question: What will these meter maids be called?) A total ban on this sound would not come free, though, for the horn does serve some purpose. Otherwise why do you pay for a horn on your car? It can be used as a warning device. If it's used too little, more accidents will occur, so obviously we should make sure there's some blowing around.

The same cannot be said for car and motorcycle exhaust systems, so there will be little cost to others if drivers are forced by law to keep their spent gases quiet. (Blind pedestrians will have a rougher time crossing streets, though.) Perhaps cars and bikes are a little more expensive with effective mufflers installed and also a little less powerful, but that's just tough, bikeboys. Why shouldn't you guys pay the price of not bothering everyone else within two miles of your hog? We won't make you pay $1000 for a perfectly silent muffler, but we should make you buy a reasonably quiet one.

The same argument holds true for construction equipment users. You can't expect the Capitalists who make air compressors and bulldozers to build quiet ones, because that would cost more. Since nobody now makes the companies who actually use the noisy equipment pay for all the noise pollution they cause, no company would pay extra for quieter machines. That's just the nature of our profit system. You seem to like to get houses, streets, all that as cheap as possible. More expensive, quieter machinery would end up costing you, so unless you're directly affected by the noise, you don't gripe at all.

We've got to make construction companies either pay off all the people they're bugging with noisy machinery, or tax them because they insist on annoying people with unwanted sound. If the tax is high enough, you can be sure air compressors will not be bothering people in the future. (On the other hand, the people affected might try bribing the noise makers.)

There will again be a cost involved. Quieter machinery will cost more, so Capitalist exploiters will end up charging more for construction. Apartments, houses, and offices will all cost more. Why shouldn't they? All the people who've been bothered by noise from this construction have actually been footing part of the bill. I see no reason why they should continue to do so instead of those of you who will use the buildings.

What about noisy dishwashers, vacuum cleaners, and garbage disposals? Believe it or not, nothing should be done about them, so long as the neighbors aren't disturbed. The user bears the full cost of the noise from household appliances. If your old lady doesn't mind all the racket, then who am I to tell her she should buy a better, quieter, more expensive vacuum cleaner? Peace is not free. People who don't want to pay the extra price shouldn't be forced to as long as no one else is involved.

Along the same lines, I don't want to make people pay more for quiet apartments unless they want to. Yes, I know, Capitalist apartment builders use the shoddiest building materials they can get away with. If they have the choice between putting up papier mâché walls or thick soundproofed ones, they'll probably choose the former, if that's what sells the best. Some apartments are soundproofed, but they cost more than the others. You can choose what you want, depending on how much you value silence relative to your total income. But poor people can't afford expensive soundproofed apartments, you say? Right. If you're really worried, give them more money directly and then let *them* decide if they are willing to pay the price for tranquility. But don't force the cost on them by passing an ordinance requiring foot-thick walls in all buildings as New York City did in 1969. Some people, poor and rich alike, don't care who hears them balling. Anyway, do *you* always close the bedroom window on those seductively warm nights?

What about all the ear-splitting noise in today's factories? Should we pass laws enforcing a maximum noise level in all manufacturing plants? If we do, you can be sure of one thing: The price of goods now made in many factories will end up costing *you* more. You're probably tempted to think that's okay since workers are paying some of the cost because they're going deaf while making these products.

But when you think about it for a while, *you're* really already paying that cost of the effects of noise on the workers. Look at it this way. Once in a while employers need more workers. When they try to hire, they offer only what they think they have to to get enough new help. But working conditions are an important part of the total pay that prospective employees look at. Some won't work in a noisy place unless they're paid something extra. When you multiply this example by the whole economy, you find that in the long run products that require the same labor and materials, but are made with noisy machinery, end up costing more because higher wages are paid to the workers making them. Even when workers know noise can hurt them, they don't always use the ear-covers provided by their employers. A GM assembly-line worker was asked why he didn't protect his ears. His answer to the reporter was, "What are you, some kind of Commie?"

You can lead a horse to grass, but you can't make him roll a joint.

THE AMERICAN WAY OF DYING

          Man has to be the most ingenious of beasts. He invented death by noise: The victim was placed inside a large bell while it was vigorously struck. He invented the wheel: The victim was strapped down on the spokes and all the bones in his body were broken with a lead pipe. He invented the rack: The victim was stretched to death. He invented the horseless carriage: Millions of victims are tortured by smog, noise, fatal and maiming accidents, and eventually premature death due to lung disease.

Isn't man fantastic?

How did we let things get to the point where 55,000 Americans are killed in cars each year; where over 80 percent of all air pollution is automobile induced; where our land is half eaten up by roads, parking lots, 220,000 hideous gas stations; where traffic noise makes city streets unbearable?

True, we might have some problems if the engine on wheels had never been invented. The throughput of a horse isn't too much trouble for a farmer with forty acres. But put everyone on horseback and cities might not be too amenable for anybody except road apple gourmets. The stories about cities back in the good old days aren't too encouraging: greenish "swirl" a half a foot deep in the streets, sidewalks too slippery to walk on, and walls splattered with the spray off carriage wheels. Dudes of those times didn't buy high boots just to be fashionable. But the saving grace of horsepower back then was that the pollution was biodegradable. Nature can take care of horseshit, eventually, but carshit is another problem altogether. In fact it might be leading us to the edge of world destruction.

When that old Chevy V-8 is fired up, one by-product from the internal combustion engine is CO_2. Hundreds of millions of tons of that invisible stuff are spewed into our atmosphere every year. The world has witnessed a fantastic increase of CO_2 in the last hundred years. If the trend continues at this rate, watch out, because carbon dioxide lets the sun in but not out. Result: Aside from a field day for sunworshippers and a lot faster growing plant life (really), melting glaciers and the return of Noah.

How are going to stop all the destruction caused by cars? Why did it happen in the first place? You guessed it. Pig Capitalists out trying to screw the public. Some cat hits the jackpot in his basement and invents an internal combustion engine. Looks like it'd work better than steam. Piggies see dollar signs. The next thing you know the assembly lines are putting out eight million smogging death traps. Piggies aren't going to waste money on anything unless they have to, right? Why should a Capitalist even spend a mere 39¢ on a smog control device if he's not required to, that is, if no car buyers demand it and no laws require him to put it in the cars he's making?

Aha, but why don't people who buy cars demand smogless engines, you say? The answer is easy. Most people, including you, prefer to buy cars that have smog-creating engines rather than smogless ones. Why? Simple. Because the former are cheaper and also require less upkeep. (Is your smog control device still connected?) You don't think GM is going to give antismog devices away free, do you? (If you do, start reading this book from the beginning.)

But everyone knows that the present auto exhaust makes for unbreathable air and all the health complications resulting. That should be ample enough incentive, right? Wrong. My van contributes only an infinitesimal bit to total air pollution. And anyway, nobody is checking up on all the smog my engine puts out or anything else that floats out of my star-spangled wonder. So it's in my own interest to buy a car without smog controls that costs less bread. Since I'm an SOB, I can in effect impose part of the cost of driving on other people. They'd have a hard time trying to contract with me not to, unless they did it collectively à la legislation or taxation. You act exactly the same way that I do.

The latter solution is what has to happen. Take, for example, ethyl gas additives. It's well known that lead in gas causes a horrible amount of pollution when it's burned in your car's engine. The threat of government legislation against lead additives pushed oil companies to offer leadless juice. And auto Capitalists promised that 90 percent of their new cars would be redesigned to accept leadless gas. Great. But not for gas dealers. After the initial fury for the stuff wore off, one dealer claimed that leadless gas was evaporating faster than he was selling it. The reason this is really happening is not hard to figure out. The cost of processing and marketing the new juice led Piggies to charge one to three cents more per gallon for it than for leading regular gas. That may not mean much to many drivers, but some won't pay the higher price.

Absurd, you say. Drivers don't know what price they're paying for gas. A survey of drivers in one area revealed just that; most said they didn't know how much they paid for juice. Funny thing, though, a study in the same location showed that gas stations charging higher prices didn't get as many customers as those stations that charged less. Why? Because although the *average* driver may not know what he's paying for gas, *some* do. They hustle to get the best deal. Gas station Capitalists who charge too much over their competition end up with not as many sales and not as much profit. You see to that if you're at all cost conscious.

If leaded gas causes lots of shit in the air, tax the shit out of leaded gas. But both Pig Capitalists in the U.S. Chamber of Commerce and workers in the AFL-CIO are against this tax. A labor spokesman said the tax "would be a license to pollute if you pay the price." But that's the whole idea. You *should* pay the full cost of all your high octane. And, besides, the tax on leaded gas will force competing Capitalists to come up with engines that work well without lead additives.

41

The ethyl tax is going to cause some of you some problems. After all, lead wasn't added to juice just for psychic kicks. You don't pay higher prices for premium just because you like the name. Lead allows high-performance engines to operate without knocking. Taxing lead will cause engines to knock in those cars whose owners feel they can no longer afford to pay the tax. They'll use regular gas and suffer. But that's just the price society will have to pay to get Detroit to improve engines.

When you get right down to it, getting a smogless mode of transportation won't be free. You're taking advantage of the cheapest means present technology can provide, given the incentives facing you and the auto makers. Change those incentives and you and technology will eventually adapt. The threat of a ban on internal combustion engines has finally prompted the invention of a viable external combustion engine. Super Capitalist Bill Lear promised to have his commercially usable steamer on the road in 1971. And the Nippon Capitalists already have a prototype steam Datson.

Why did these Piggies wait until the internal combustion engine had already screwed everything up? Simple, you the consumer until now haven't had to pay the social costs of driving, only the private costs (gas, depreciation, repairs). New legislation is forcing auto makers to pass on the cost of keeping the air clean to consumers. Competition among Piggies is forcing them to seek the lowest cost method of pollution control for the rolling coffins they sell. That may mean changes in internal combustion engines or a switch to some sort of smogless steam engine. The only thing you've got to remember is that perhaps you can get GM to pay for part of the cost of cleaning up car smoke because of all the monopoly profits it may be making. But anybody who drives is going to end up paying most of the price of smogless wheels. That's fine with me—from each according to how much he's screwing the environment.

Nothing has been said about GM putting out so many cars that are unsafe. Ralph Nader finally showed the world the conspiracy going on among auto makers to prevent Americans from riding in safe cars. How did GM get away with it for so long? Who was aiding and abetting the enemy?

Guess who. It was you! You're immediately going to say Angus doesn't know the difference between his ass and a hot rock. I do mix them up occasionally, but I still know that Capitalists are out to make as much bread as possible. If enough of you really wanted to drive safe cars, why didn't GM, Ford, or Chrysler, or American Motors, or Volkswagen, or Toyota, or Fiat attempt to cash in on your demands many years back? Actually in '58 Ford tried to sell safety and lost its shirt in the process—nobody wanted to buy. GM sells you a $3000 coffin with 455 hp. because that's how GM makes the most bucks. You're the ones who want to spend your money on flashy fastbacks that are relatively unsafe; otherwise some foxy Capitalist would be selling you something else.

But why can't we have flashy cars which are also safe? We can, at a price. Installing safety features costs manufacturers. Are they going to give them to you gratis? They'd sell their sow for a quarter; charity is definitely not a Piggy's trip.

Since safety costs money, auto buyers like you haven't wanted to pay for it in the past. And if individual drivers were the only ones getting killed by their own recklessness, my comment would be that that's their hang up. Why should I make a dude pay for a collapsible steering column if he doesn't want it? It's his right to be suicidal. Also, if liability for accidents were perfect, I wouldn't care if the dude could buy a car with no brakes. He'd have to pay the full cost of his actions if he took unwilling bystanders along on his short-cut to Nirvana.

Before you call me a murderer of priceless human lives, look at your own actions. Do you consider your life priceless? Maybe, but certainly you do not run your life as if you do. Is all of your income spent protecting your precious body? Don't you ever speed? Don't you ever fly in planes? Don't you ever put off going to a doctor when something is bothering you? Have you *never* taken mescaline just because *some* of it is cut with strychnine? You don't value your life at ∞; why should I? Why should people be forced to spend more for their own well being than they choose to?

The same argument holds for the quality aspects of the cars people buy. Right now, irritated Congressmen are complaining that cars are made for style and not durability. Auto insurance companies are so pissed off they're about to break up the marriage with GM, et al. Dr. William Hadden, Jr., head of the Insurance Highway Safety Institute, calculates that repair costs traceable to many of today's auto designs "are levying a tax on the motoring public now running $10 billion a year."

By now you should be able to recognize that Mr. Hadden's argument is full of unadulterated fecal matter (no preservative added). People who buy cars obviously prefer a slick design at the lowest price possible rather than a more expensive, more damage-proof set of wheels. Costs of insurance and repair are such right now that people are willing to pay for them and pay less for chintzy sleekness. Remember, crush resistant bumpers aren't free and don't look as good as the useless ornaments that now hardly pass off as same. Detroit is out to make bread, the more the better. You start demanding crumple-resistant bumpers and GM will give them to you —at a price, of course. It's your choice, not auto Capitalist's or the Government's.

Ours is a world of trade-offs. Once you realize *that* you'll see how most of what our government is regulating ends up making some people pay for what they don't want to spend their money on. If I'm forced to pay all that money for a Sherman Tank to drive the expressways, I probably won't have enough bread left over to get me any decent shit. How will I get off then?

7.

POWER TO THE PEDESTRIAN

Detroit has pushed off so many tin monsters on us that the cities are being strangled to death. It's so bad in some places that walking is almost as impossible as driving. Solution: Give the streets back to the people. New Yorkers saw how great it was on Fifth Avenue during Earth Day. Tokyo prevented wheels on the Ginza after the city almost dropped dead when fumes from 2,000,000 cars were trapped overhead by a temperature inversion. The ban on cars brought about by that close call showed the Japanese how great life in the city can be without automobiles. Germany has at least thirty *Fussgängerstrassen,* pedestrian streets; and Italy has many "pedestrian islands."

Fussgängerstrassen are simple to create, so why all the fuss about cars congesting downtown streets? Well, when you prevent cats from tooling around some streets they will simply pile up on others. Obviously there are just too many cars in the city. The reason is clear: You find that cars are a better deal than any substitute. And, besides, you don't have to pay all the costs. When you pull on to Madison Avenue during the rush hour, you don't have to pay all the other dudes who go slower because of your car. And you don't have to pay all those who don't even try to drive on that street because they know it's going to be crowded. You don't yet pay for all the foul vapors your 450 hp. V-8 puts in the air.

Changing our congested cities into pedestrian paradises may seem like a great idea, but it's certainly not obvious that we'd all be better off. Let's face it, you like driving a car, and you'd suffer if cars were *never* allowed in the city.

Instead of eliminating city cars completely, we could just make motorists pay the full cost of driving there. Just bill them according to the amount of driving they do, when they do it, and where. How? With T.V. activated computer billing machines. Really, it could work, except the Feds would use the information to bring 1984 closer.

The charges would be different for driving at 2:00 A.M. than at 5:00 P.M. At two in the morning there's no congestion. Motorists aren't slowing anyone down; most of them are at home getting a little peace. At five in the evening, it's a different story, so make drivers pay accordingly. The same goes for toll bridges. At rush hours, charge more than at other times. Ever wonder why it takes so long to get over so many toll bridges at 5:00 P.M.? Well, instead of making people pay more for crowding up the bridges then, many benevolent cities charge them less, via commuter tickets. That kind of pricing has to be insane. After all, if you choose to drive the bridge at 5:00 P.M., you're making others pay in lost time because you cause them to go slower. Why should you be rewarded by getting a book of tickets that lets you pay less?

Look at our cities' freeways and expressways. Are they crowded all the time? Hardly, but we're told we've got to lay out more taxes to pay for more roads. Why should I pay one cent for more freeways that will be full only part of the time? Why should I pay for dudes to drive all by themselves at rush hours in twenty-two-foot long Cadillacs and Lincolns? Since we don't make them pay the full price of cruising on the freeways, they don't make much attempt to rearrange their hours or to reduce crowding by driving in car pools or taking buses.

I have a solution for expressway congestion. Every cat caught at the wheel during the rush hour without three passengers will be fined $100. Try that on for size and see how many more freeways will "have" to be built because we "desperately" need more of them.

If the auto company stooges succeed in getting your city to, nonetheless, put up some new freeways, at least make sure that those who are shafted get fully compensated. Freeways have a nasty habit of going right through poor peoples' neighborhoods. The value of their houses fall; they get taken. They should be fully paid for the losses they sustain.

Where will the money come from? Part of it will be taxed away from all the rich suburban property owners whose land values go up because of the new freeway. The rest should come from all those benefited by being able to get into town faster. (That's why suburban property values went up in the first place.)

It's only fair. Some of you may ask, why build anything at all for cars? Why not rapid transit? As the chief economist for the Czechago Area Transportation Study has said: "Urban mass transportation in the United States is in the early stages of a vast transformation, a transformation that will rival the rags-to-riches changes visited upon a fairy tale Cinderella."

Well, to the chagrin of many, mass transit to date is still a fairy tale and a demented one at that.

San Francisco's BART will require an annual subsidy equal to twice the total fare it collects. It will do nothing for the poor and autoless, who live near the city's center. BART doesn't come near very many low-income districts; when it does, the stations are so far apart that people have to drive to get to them. That's a big help.

In D.C. on the Shirly Highway, superfast transit buses are the only vehicles allowed on two full lanes. The result: 40 percent of the highway is used to carry 19 percent of the traffic because not enough commuters want to take the bus. Do you, even when the alternative is there?

Flint, Michigan, got about $1½ million from our magnanimous government (your taxes, brothers and sisters) to make twenty-six buses into luxury hotels on wheels. These maxiliners tool through the suburbs in search of passengers. Inside there's air-conditioning, music, big seats, everything a commuter could dream of, except maybe a piece of ass. At last report Flint was losing $5200 a day in its newest rapid transit invention.

Recent elections have seen voters turn down bond issues for proposed rapid transit systems in Seattle and other cities.

What's the problem? Are we doomed to an automobile society or will we ever wise up and leave the driving to someone else? You can be sure we won't until motorists are forced to pay the full cost of driving. You can be sure that mass transit is doomed as long as the auto remains the most heavily subsidized beast in the nation. People aren't going to give up the convenience of a private car until they're forced to. We'll force them by sticking them with the cost of all the highway destruction, of all the air pollution, of all the noise, and of all the congestion that they cause.

Even then we still might not see rapid transit put Detroit out of business. It may turn out that even when all the costs are laid on you, you'll still prefer to drive your own car. Then you'll have no one to blame for car-produced evils except yourself, which is true even now.

DROP THE BIRTH RATE
OR DROP DEAD

A hundred bodies to every square yard of space on this earth in the year 2870. Not a pleasant thought, is it? Probably wouldn't want to wish such a fate on a government bureaucrat, let alone your own people. No amount of good weed would get you to adjust to such overcrowding. Megadeaths are okay for Herman Kahn's demented mind, but megalives are certainly not what we should be pushing onto our grandchildren.

The population growth in some countries already equals their increase in output so that nobody, except a few modern-day patricians, gets any better off in these places. Obviously those screwed-up countries can't even afford the luxury of worrying about pollution problems. They're still trying to get off their treadmills.

One of America's greatest minds, Paul Ehrlich, knows what the problem is—"the human population of the planet is about five times too large, and we're managing to support all these people—at today's level of misery—only by spending our capital, burning our fossil fuels, dispensing our mineral resources and turning our fresh water into salt water."

The solution: Get the U.S. population down to 50,000,000, the world's down to a half billion. Nice thought, Paul, but there are some problems with getting the U.S. down to manageable size. Right now there are about one and a half cities in the U.S. that can support good movies, big bookstores, live theater, and decent rock shows. Turns out that certain kinds of specialization depends on how many people are around. Everybody likes the idea of having lots of culture, but do you see much of it in small towns? No chance, because it can't survive. Cut the big cities to pieces and you won't even find pieces of many of those cherished leisure-time activities that are now available.

And has our celebrated biologist ever considered what would happen to the age structure of America if we cut the population by 75 percent? Right now the median age is about twenty-seven years. It's been steadily declining as our population has been growing. If we were merely to stabilize, that is, have a zero growth rate, the median age would jump about ten years. Now hold on. Think what the age structure would be if we dropped down to fifty million inhabitants.

Assuming we accomplished this insane feat via birth control and not death uncontrol, we would live through a good many decades with the median age of the population far in excess of that which exists with a stable population. The thought of an America filled more and more with social security cases and less and less with young bloods makes me rather uneasy. Is that the kind of situation you would want to live in?

Well, let's forget all that kind of crap and concentrate on the real problem—keeping the population from exploding, not imploding. I suggest universal sterilization—every citizen choosing his own ways and means. Actually we can make dudes effectively cut the cord simply by taxing the sperm out of couples with more than two kids (if we're really sure that people shouldn't be allowed to have so many kids). After all, kids are just a consumer good from which parents derive their kicks. Raise the price of kids, and parents will buy less, that is, ball less and/or use better birth control methods and/or have abortions. We could do that easily now just by eliminating tax deductions parents can use if they have kids.

Anyway, if birth control were more sure and more widely-used, and abortion everywhere legal, safe, and cheap, we might not ever have to apply the baby tax. A recent study at Princeton University indicated that unwanted births accounted for 35 to 45 percent of the increase in population between 1960 and 1968. No more unwanted babies means less body growth in America. So why aren't we helping people prevent little kids from exiting into our already mixed-up world?

The Catholic Church is one reason. Being against abortion, the Pill, and all except filtertip condoms, Popes for centuries have kept an iron hand on off the seminal intake of the world's tubes. And in the U.S. many of our friendly congressmen have quietly kept the government from helping along the birth-control cause. In 1970 House Speaker McCormack worked to bury the Senate-approved $1 billion birth control bill. With a name like that, no wonder. In general, governments have spent their energies in death control, but birth control seemed too touchy a subject to spend money on.

The battle against abortion has been fought even more overtly. A few states at best legally permit abortion on demand. Many chicks don't want kids, but get k.u.'d anyway. If they're rich, they can get an abortion anywhere. If they're poor, they get the back-of-the-barber-shop special and end up in the hospital with a punctured uterus or worse. As with so many other things, the poor just get screwed and the rich get screwed and still get what they want.

Even in New York, where abortion can be had on demand, the poor get shafted, for only fetus removals done in the hospital are legal. You gotta pay for the hospital, and at today's prices that ain't peanuts. What a lot of bull. Midwives deliver kids around the world, but much simpler abortions must be done here by M.D.'s in expensive hospitals. Any nurse who can operate a vacuum cleaner can now perform a safe fifteen-minute abortion. It's as if there were a conspiracy between hospitals and rich doctors.

So we repeal all abortion laws, make the Pill available without prescription, educate our teenieboppers into the ways of safe fornication. Will we be on the road to zero population growth? Not according to Ehrlich and crew. But perhaps biologists should learn to read numbers better.

The birth rate in the U.S. is near its record low: We simply didn't continue breeding like in the silent fifties. (Now you know why people were so quiet then.) In fact, if I were to do as Ehrlich does and simply project trends blindly into the future, I'd predict a zero birth rate in little more than twenty years. The Census Bureau tells us that the ratio of children born to women in their fertile years is now the lowest it's been since World War II.

And anyway, is America overcrowded? England has 588 people per square mile, Holland 975. Compare those with the U.S.—56 per square mile. Some countries are even concerned about too *little* population growth. For example, since 1964 the rate of growth of France's population has fallen so much that the Frogs are worried about an eventual excess of inactive old-age people over and above the number of so-called active citizens. France has been fighting this problem since 1943 by giving special family allowances to encourage more kids. The government there is now thinking about even bigger allowances to fight the continually falling birth rate. The population explosion, Dr. Erhlich, is not by any means worldwide.

And even if population stops growing in the U.S., do you think that will stop pollution? If you do, you're as freaked out as our misguided biologist. Put enough resources at one man's disposal and he would pollute the whole mother country. Pollution comes from the *use* of resources, not the mere existence of people. Cut the U.S. population to 50,000,000 people and I guarantee you that, if they have enough income, they will be able to pollute just as much as the present 200,-000,000 Americans are doing. Pollution won't stop with a stalled population, unless people are prevented from consuming. Pollution can be stopped only by making people pay the full cost of their actions. You know that every extra dollar you can get your hands on is usually spent. Do you ever wonder about all the extra pollution caused by all the new things you buy? Probably not. You may not know it, but every time you go up a little bit on the income ladder you end up contributing more pollution to our environment. And I'll bet you wouldn't have it any other way, because higher incomes seem to make people like you happier.

Now look at destruction by robbery and murder. It isn't necessarily caused by too much population. Britain has a population density ten times ours, but has fewer murders in the whole country than Richard Daley's little empire has.

If you live in a city like N.Y.C. or L.A. or S.F. or Chicago, you may think there's a population problem. But that certainly isn't the case for North Dakota, South Dakota, or Wyoming. Those states actually *lost* population from 1960 to 1970, and are quite upset about it.

If crowded cities are so bad, why are you in one? And nobody is forcing all those cats to move away from the Dakotan toolies. Big cities obviously offer enough benefits to outweigh the misery of smoggy air, deafening noise, congestion, and, in short, of the whole rotten mess. How many of you are reading this while sitting in your house in the country with never a manhole near?

If there's really a population problem in the U.S. it must reside in the minds of publicity-hungry academics. India, Japan, China, and other places do have something to worry about. Why should *you* worry about it? The next time someone tells you not to have more than two kids, tell him to keep track of his own sperm, not yours.

WATER, WATER EVERYWHERE,
BUT NOT A DROP TO DRINK

One of nature's most precious resources is going down the drain, never to return in its pure state again. Things have gotten a little better; once upon a time, in most places, you could watch feces floating by on your local river. The situation has not improved everywhere. More than 1400 communities in the U.S. still dump untreated excremental matter into their waterways. Even big cities like Memphis do it. And every Pig Capitalist in the land dumps as much industrial sewage as he needs to into any adjacent river or lake. Runoff from all the years and years of using chemical fertilizer is poisoning our water even more.

A recent study showed that several million Americans drink water containing hazardous amounts of chemicals or biological contamination. That funny taste in your glass could be fecal bacteria, lead, arsenic, barium, cadmium, chromium, or selenium—all in potentially dangerous amounts. It's enough to turn a man into a wino.

And to top it all off, some cities actually run out of what now passes for water during the summer. Remember the pictures of dry fountains in New York City during the hot summer days? Why did New York have a water crisis? Because Piggies were destroying all the good water? Perhaps, in part, but only a small part. There were other reasons, and you're one of the biggest ones if you experienced the misfortune of living in N.Y.C. then. It so happened that water use wasn't metered. That meant that it didn't pay you to fix leaks, to turn off the water while shaving, to cut back on quenching the thirst of a large lawn.

But water is essential, so it should be free, you say. Now what kind of intestinal overflow is that? Doesn't it cost money to bring water from rivers and lakes into your apartment or house? Even if the water isn't being used by anyone on a lake, that doesn't mean it's free to use from your faucet. Since somebody has to pay for the pipes and pumps and reservoirs so that you can have running water, how can you expect it to be free? If you decide to have a huge lawn that you put tons of water on every week, why, please tell me, should the rest of us pay for any part of it?

So, the solution to New York's water shortage must have

been obvious. Well, it wasn't. Instead of making you pay directly for wasting water by charging according to metered use, the lords running the city decided to deceive the public by making everyone pay for all the wasted water. How? By having a dam built to supply more water for every rich bastard's big lawn and all those extra-long showers you like to take. The cost? Only ten times what it would have been if meters had been installed.

Once you realize that water really isn't free, then you can readily understand that purity in water isn't necessarily free either. People wastes have to end up somewhere. Where does this stuff go? Eventually, it will end up in a body of water and it keeps coming down. To keep the water pure, somebody's got to filter out raw sewage, and that costs money. You've got to pay for it one way or another, either through higher taxes for filtration systems or through impure water. If your water isn't pure, then it's up to you to demand to pay higher taxes to clean it up. Will you do it?

If your town is upstream, you can dump into the downstream towns. It's cheaper for you, but that's dirty pool. All cities should be required to bear the burden of their own lumpy waste.

Everyone agrees with this when it's a question of factories dumping their crap into rivers and lakes, so why not apply the same rules to human sewage? Crap by any other name pollutes the same, except along the shores of Connecticut and Lake Michigan.

What? Daley knows how to nullify pollution in his serfdom's lake? Hardly! He just makes sure that his South Side beaches aren't closed down in spite of the health hazards the putrid water presents. He's no fool. After all, keep the natives cool and avoid riots. The same holds true for many polluted beaches in Connecticut. Blacks will have to start dropping dead when they hit the water before sharp politicians will close off such a cheap form of hot summers' riot control.

And the Pig Capitalist polluters should be so lucky as to locate their plants on the water near a ghetto; it will be a long time before they're forced to do anything about all the wastes they dump into the surrounding waters.

Not being satisfied with merely dumping poison in rivers and lakes, Piggies are ruining the ecology with hot water. A hot bath on your body is nice for you, but that's not the best aquatic trip for marine life, except algae. Green slime thrives on a nice warm environment, especially if some good shit, like phosphates, is present.

The worst offenders are the big thermal nuclear power plants. But you can't get the Piggies running them to admit that they're destroying the adjacent aquatic environment. Du-Pont Co. even claims that thermal pollution not only doesn't harm fish but actually helps them. DuPont says that the lake at their Savannah River plant has bigger and faster-growing turtles and bigger and faster-growing fish than lakes that aren't heated up. DuPont says that swimmers like warm water better than cold. DuPont is trying to tell conservationists that maybe thermal pollution isn't so bad after all. DuPont is trying to tell conservationists that the problem should be studied more. But why should conservationists study the problem more when they already know the answer?

Nuclear power plants provide you with relatively inexpensive electricity, so you probably would not lift a finger to get rid of them, even if it were proven that the thermal pollution they cause destroys the surrounding ecology. And, anyway, if given the choice between regular air polluting electricity generation and nuclear generation, which one would you pick? Don't answer like a typical mother country radical and say neither because both forms change the ecology. You like living with lots of cheap power. There's still no way for us to get it without some amount of pollution. The choice can only be made about which is the best source of power after you've examined all the benefits and all the costs.

BROWNOUT

Until recently the above word would have been unknown to all but a small band of Arab preverts. Now it's the latest rage: The lights get a little bit dimmer; the air conditioning puts out a little less cool air; and factories turn out almost obsolete products at a little slower clip. In case you can't see your newspaper we're suffering from a power crisis.

But how can that be? The ads tell us to live better electrically. The electric company gives us a special low rate if we use more electricity every month? Who's putting who on?

I'd say it's Con Ed and Brothers who are putting all of us on. The facts speak for themselves.

In July 1970 one-third of New York's subways were sidelined because of a power shortage that hit the entire Northeast. N.Y. Telephone had to switch on its own 35,000 KW. emergency generating capacity. American Express shut off all its air conditioners during a turn of 90° weather. Sixty-two elevators were shut down at Rockefeller Center.

In August of 1970 Con Ed was forced to cut back voltage by 8 percent. The brownout had its effect! Hospital operations had to be postponed; air conditioners had their motors ruined; the tube went fuzzy.

What's the problem? Con Ed will tell you it was caused by a few broken generators and a greedy public using "too much" electricity. Bull! What are you supposed to do, not put on the air conditioner and then roast in 90° heat? The real problem lies elsewhere, as we'll see.

There's no doubt we live in an electric society: electric power motors, electric garage doors, electric toothbrushes, electric combs, electric vibrators. We have been badgered into thinking that electricity would always be there; Reddy Kilowatt at your service forever more.

Now we hear a different tune. "What we have is a crisis amid abundance," declares one staffee of the White House Science and Tech Office. "Lack of energy is going to start inhibiting our economic growth and perhaps our standard of living," proclaims a vice-president of a large corporation.

"You may see some industries that will be operating [only] seven or eight months a year due to energy shortages," maintains an official of Armco Steel.

For once, Piggies are running scared, but so, too, are consumers. When the juice stops flowing, the lights go out everywhere.

I guarantee you though that there's an easy solution to the energy shortage. Simply raise the price. Ridiculous? Think about it. If there's not enough juice for everyone at the going price, it means that when you turn on the stereo, someone else can't get as much power. Why shouldn't you have to pay for perhaps causing your neighbor's Mixmaster to slow down because you caused the electricity to be cut back? And when a Piggie starts up his air-conditioning unit in the plant to keep his slaves from revolting, why shouldn't he have to pay the full cost of the power he uses? That cost includes taking power away from somebody else.

What's happening now is really a pretty half-assed scheme—asking some people to stop using their electric goodies, cutting off power to some plants, reducing voltage to parts of the country once in a while. Besides being unworkable and arbitrary, that kind of rationing nonsense went out with the days of price controls. Just get the utilities to raise their prices so that you are eventually forced to decide not to "waste" electricity anymore. Then there won't be any shortages—no more brownouts, blackouts, and arbitrary energy cutoffs.

But the price of electricity shouldn't be raised across the

board. During some times of the day there are unused supplies, while at other times no more extra juice can flow because full capacity has been reached. The utility companies
should charge a high price during these periods and a low
price at other times. It's really the only sensible thing to do.

But you don't like the idea of high electricity bills. Tough
shit. You're already paying a higher price than you think,
because brownouts and blackouts aren't costless. They cost
you in inconvenience, in more accidents because of dim
lighting, and in more expensive products because of inter-
rupted production.

You're also paying a higher price in the form of pollution
generated by power stations. You think that juice comes
from heaven? Instead, look to the sky for some extra large
billows of black coal smoke. That isn't coming from Jove.
It will either be coming from some Capitalist's steel mill or
Con Ed's generating plant.

Some utilities say they want to stop polluting, but it would
be too expensive. That's crap again. We're paying the cost
in a ruined environment now, all of us. The users of energy
are making everyone share these costs. Why not make utilities pay the price of pollution prevention? Raise the price of
juice to cover the costs, and let users of energy pay for the
full price of providing kilowatts? It's only fair.

Every once in a while some prophet of doom from a large
power company makes a public statement that the end has
come. A spokesman for American Electric Power once declared that coal stocks at its power plants were "dangerously
low," and that "in some cases, adequate supplies are unob-
tainable virtually at any price." Pure nonsense. I'm sure,
Mr. American Electric, that at a high enough price you'd

get all of the world's coal delivered to your doorstep wrapped with a big red ribbon. What the badass means is he doesn't want to pay more than he's used to for black diamonds. He even suggested that exports of our coal be restricted so that more would be available for domestic electricity generation. Why should American Electric Power get coal at a price lower than what the black stuff's worth? Why should workers in the coal mines get lower pay (because the value of their product is lower) just so those who want cheap energy can get it? Coal producers aren't placing "fuel requirements of foreign countries" ahead of supplying a "vital public source at home." Coal Piggies are after all the bread they can get, as usual. They don't care about public service, and neither does the president of any power company. Once you realize that all those dudes are out only to make their own lives happy, then you won't ask for "public service" solutions to economic problems. In fact, you'd probably get a better deal if you forced your state to relinquish its regulation of those power companies. When a utility is regulated, the cats running the show try to keep the boat from rocking, try to make life easy for themselves. How much efficiency can we expect in such a situation?

When utilities complain they can't buy clean-burning natural gas to run their generators, they're probably right. But what's the difference between buying coal and buying natural gas? The former is not a regulated industry, but the latter most certainly is.

The production, shipment, and pricing of natural gas is totally regulated by government flunkies. There really is a shortage of clean-burning natural gas, but it exists only because these regulators won't let gas companies raise their rates. Since gas firms haven't been making much money lately, they haven't expanded their supplies. And since many fuel users think that natural gas is so cheap, they want to buy lots of it. Hence, a shortage.

Commonwealth Edison wants to buy lots and lots of clean-burning natural gas as part of its antipollution trip. But Peoples Gas doesn't want to sell much to the utility company. Peoples Gas wants to establish different priorities of classes, and ration accordingly. That's insane. Let natural gas flow to places where its value to society is highest. If electricity generation is one of them, then utility companies will be willing to pay the price. Keeping the price down on natural gas just screws up the works and only benefits those lucky gas users who get a ration ticket for some of the available supplies. And even then they might prefer to pay a higher price and get all they want, instead of the paltry amount currently available.

You're probably thinking now that rationing of such an irreplaceable resource as natural gas is a good thing. After all, if we use it up any faster we'll run out faster and then the shit will really hit the hippo's tail.

Old myths die hard, but I must tell you something. If Piggies own the gas resources, do you think they'll give the stuff away? Don't you think they are going to try to make as much bread as possible? They will estimate what reserves will be in the future as opposed to what the demand will be. You can believe that they'll take just enough gas out of the ground so that they get the most profit from these reserves. If regulation of gas price and of production is removed, we'll probably see prices rising and production increasing. Since so many people are cooking with gas, and others want to but can't, unregulated gas companies could raise prices and still sell a lot of the colorless stuff. They'd be making more bucks so they'd want to make even more by looking for and tapping new reserves. But then we'll run out of gas sooner. So what? What good does it do us in the ground? In fact, let's say using one cubic foot of gas could produce $50,000 worth of machinery. Then I'd say use up all the gas immediately. We'll have a higher standard of living and so will our gasless grandchildren.

11.

WASHDAY WONDERS --
FOOD FOR STARVING ALGAE.

Could it be that Pig Capitalists peddling detergents actually have a soft spot in their hearts? Do they really feel sorry for undernourished algae? Is that why they decided to put phosphates in their washday miracles, so that all the green slime in all the lakes could get a rich diet of such a needed nutrient when the human pollutants run out?

Since Piggies couldn't give a damn about starving humans,

it's hard to imagine they really wanted to help out the algae population. The effects of their rapacious greed and all you fastidious housewives together have fed the algae to gluttony.

There're so many profit seekers trying to make a buck that they grab onto any new idea that will help them sell their products. Stooge scientists discovered that sodium tripolyphosphate, when added to detergent, softened the water and fairly plucked out the dirt from grandma's drawers. Soon every soap in town had a "miracle additive" that got whites whiter. (Who ever thinks white is beautiful these days anyway?)

You have to realize that the only reason "miracle additives" *were* added is because you wanted them. They aren't a fiction created by Madison Avenue. Any housewife can tell whether or not they made a significant difference. They apparently did because no detergent was able to survive on the market without additives. Don't play the innocent, Mrs. Ameriᴋᴋᴋan Housewife; you like whites whiter.

Piggies failed (or did they?) to realize that detergent residue ends up in our streams and lakes. The new phosphate additive turned out to be just the right kind of diet for algae. Fields of green ooze flourish on the stuff. All lakes with large phosphate content can support lots of plant life. Great for the plants, but not so great for fish. You see, when a lake has lots of algae the slime gets attacked by bacteria, which in the process uses up all the oxygen in the water. The unlucky lake gets filled with leeches (as the Captain of the *African Queen* once muddily complained: "If there's one thing I can't stand, it's leeches.") slug worms, scavenger fish, and eventually the whole mess turns into a swamp. No more swimming; no more fishing.

Well, now that you know what your box of Tide XK or

Breeze is doing to the lakes around you, will you stop using them? A few of you might try, but the rest will go on as before. After all, you don't contribute *that* much to the whole slimy mess when you wash your Levi's out, so why should *you* alone do anything about it? And why should Piggies take sodium tripolyphosphate out of their products? If one manufacturer did, he'd lose a little business, so fat chance, because he who pleases most sells the most products.

Since no one is forced to pay the cost of dead lakes due to detergent additives, no one will do anything about it, certainly not you.

Is a total ban on phosphates the solution? According to one of the lackeys for the Soap and Detergent Association the loss of phosphates "would be equivalent to setting back health, cleanliness and sanitation standards many years." Now you know that's a pile of algae excrement, but it is true that a ban on phosphates would impose a cost on all of you who'd like to buy such detergents until something else was invented.

Canada has already said it will prohibit the stuff by the end of '72. And the House Government Operations Committee's panel on resources has recommended that the U.S. follow suit.

This threat has caused detergent Piggies to stir a little. Their scientists have already found a substitute. It's called nitrilotriacetic acid or NTA. (Don't try it, though, for you won't get off on this acid.) Unfortunately, those little furry bastards, rats, seem to get kidney disease when they're given big doses of it. That doesn't necessarily mean that the stuff is toxic in humans, but more research could be done to find out before you sprinkle it on your Kellogg's Special K in the morning.

Sears & Roebuck claims it has the answer. A detergent without phosphate and without NTA. So you see, something else *can* be found as a substitute. The problem is getting Piggies to look for one. Unless there's an incentive, like more profits, it's not worth the hassel to them. After all, you haven't switched to pure soap for your washing, have you? Right now the incentive is provided by the probable upcoming ban on phosphates. There are also other ways. If it is established that an additive screws up our lakes, we could tax each package of soap according to how much of that particular poison is in it. Set the tax at a level which will generate enough revenue to either clean up a lot of the slime that detergent runoff causes or at least more-or-less pay off all the users of dead lakes who are the ones actually incurring the costs of the phosphates. (They could pay you *not* to use phosphate-filled detergents, but the transaction would be rather difficult, if not impossible.)

Who will pay the tax? Piggies? You can bet your sweet ass not, for the detergent business is highly competitive. Consumers of detergents will. And why shouldn't you? You're the ones using the stuff, not the Piggies. Piggies, by definition, never wash. I suspect that the tax on brands of soap using lots of phosphates will be so high that no one will buy them. Capitalists peddling Surf, Silver Dust, Oxydol, Dash, and Salvo will end up losing sales to Ivory Snow, Lux Flakes, Duz Soap, and Coldwater All. Because the latter have no phosphates and the former have the most.

If we want to see action, we've got to make people pay. If we want to see you squirm, we've got to get you where it hurts—in the wallet. Since you won't stop using washday wonders on your own accord, we'll just make it a little more individually painful to do so.

12.

HOW TO STOP ALL POLLUTION

(Please turn page)

Stop
living.

13.

OFF THE PILL

Did you know that a 1968 British study found that r.g.'s who use the Pill are seven to ten times more likely to die from blood clots than those who don't use it? Did you know that your Food and Drug Administration has records of thousands of adverse reactions to the Pill? Did you know that it wasn't until more than a year *after* Enovid was marketed that the Piggies putting it out, G.D. Searle Co., released records which showed 132 cases of blood clots and 11 deaths?

You really shouldn't be surprised. Just another case of profits over people. Why isn't our government doing anything about drug companies these days? What about all those thalidomide babies? What about the 1000 percent markup on many drugs?

Well, we do have a federal watchdog to protect us. But let's see what the FDA does with its resources. Now remember, we're going to be discussing the Food and Drug Administration, although you may not believe it.

In 1947 *The New Republic* carried an article about Dr. Wilhelm Reich, a psychoanalyst. Seems that this cat found the key to the good life—orgone, the essence of orgasm. FDA staffees didn't believe orgone accumulators, orgone blankets, and orgone boxes should be sold to the public. So for thirteen years they spent your tax money getting after Mr. Orgone himself. The FDA didn't stop at merely prohibiting the sale of orgasm essence. (Anybody know a good dealer?) It also got a court injunction prohibiting the sale of ten books by Reich.

But that wasn't enough. You thought *Fahrenheit 451* was a fantasy? Think again. In July 1956 the FDA entered Reich's home and burned his books! Reich was used to it though. His books had been burned in Germany. (Guess when?) As late as 1960 FDA'ers were still on search-and-burn missions in an attempt to destroy every last page that Reich had written.

This is straight, brothers and sisters. This story is not literary fantasia. It really happened, right here in Ameriкккa. Your tax dollars are supporting a federal agency supposedly in existence to test the food and pharmaceuticals you can buy.

But many of your tax dollars are going for that agency's Gestapo adventures instead.

What else does the FDA spend your money on? In the summer of 1970 the agency did you the big favor of banning fifteen antibiotic-combination drugs used for head colds and the like. Really, it's a big favor to you, because research showed that mixtures of antibiotics, decongestants, pain killers, and antiallergenic agents didn't offer any advantage over the components used separately.

But think about it. Why should we be spending tax dollars to find out what's a good cold tablet? Aren't there lots of companies competing in that field? Aren't they trying to take each other's customers away? And if doctors realize that, for example, TAO-AC capsules are really useless, won't they stop prescribing them?

I don't really want to have my tax dollars wasted on that kind of government research. Let the FDA check out what's dangerous, not what is or isn't a good buy. They don't have to do that, because people find out for themselves and quit buying lousy products. If companies selling those products don't make as much money on them, they may end up stopping production.

You don't believe me? Listen to a spokesman for Pfizer, Inc.: "Although the sales volume of each of these products is quite small, we are fully convinced they are effective . . . However, in view of the declining phasing demand for these two products [combination drugs] we don't plan to contest the FDA order, which would remove them from the market." And what's more, Pfizer had already stopped marketing the combo pill, TAO-AC, way before the FDA banned it! Doctors don't need to be told that a certain drug is a bad deal; they'll find out, as Pfizer, Inc., finally realized. Why waste bread with FDA to investigate, sometimes after the fact, as with TAO-AC capsules?

Does the government ever do anything good? It does test drugs for their safety aspects so that people won't drop dead from a new kind of vaccine. The Department of Health, Education and Welfare even wants us all to suffer as little pain as possible. It decided not to consider a contract bid for German measles vaccine by Phillips Roxane Laboratories, Inc. Why? Because HEW said the Roxane vaccine caused too many temporary side effects. Great, job well done.

Roxane didn't agree, but Capitalists are never happy when they can't screw the public. The president of the company, Gerald Wojtu, maintains that the side effects of his vaccine were greater than those of his two competitors, but that his drug offered more protection against reinfection.

What if he's right? Then HEW staffees made a decision for you and me. They felt that we preferred to trade off a more effective but more uncomfortable vaccine for a less effective one with fewer temporary side effects. As far as I am concerned, I'd like to have the choice. Why should some government lackey make it for me? What do you say?

Now back to the Pill. Should it be banned? Should we stop our females from being jacked up on birth control tablets? There's little doubt now that they produce side effects, even death due to blood clotting in some women. What's more, the Pill allows for dirty sex: "A promiscuous intercourse to such a degree as to prevent the birth of children seems to lower, in the most marked manner, the dignity of human nature. It cannot be without its effect on men, and nothing can be more obvious than its tendency to degrade the female character, and to destroy all its most amiable and distinguished characteristics." [1]

With so many bad aspects of the Pill, how come we allow it to be sold? In fact, why do women who know better continue taking it?

Ask them. They'll tell you it's worth the risk. That is, the benefits far outweigh the costs. Each chick can make her own utility calculations. All the government should do is provide accurate information. And if the government doesn't want to, I'm sure the condom and diaphragm makers will lend a hand. Most people value present pleasure over the slight possibility of pain in the distant future.

[1] T.R. Malthus, *An Essay on Population.*

14.

FLY THE GOLDEN BIRD
WITH THE PROUD TAIL

An ad for a high-class hooker? No, it's an ad for a high-priced combination noise maker and air polluter which incidentally doesn't get you there on time. Continental Airlines may have proud birds with golden tails, and United may fly friendly skies, but some of us on the ground are walking noisy, smoggy paths because of the air age we live in. Planes are noisy. Planes emit pollution. Right now junior executives and cross-country salesmen who fly in those planes don't pay for the destruction they're causing.

Consider the SST. It would have flown at supersonic speeds, rushing wealthy Americans to business meetings and tours of the Coliseum. The cost of developing the gem was trivial —only several billion dollars. Tricky Dick, always happy to give away tax dollars for the benefit of the rich, was trying to get Congress to pay for much of the project. Boeing's Capital Hill flunkies contended that if the SST wasn't built, thousands of jobs would be sacrificed, thousands of families would suffer.

Does that mean that all the government has to do is plow bread into any project it wants and magic, more jobs? Why, we should never have unemployment then, because all Congress has to do is keep giving money away. You know as well as I do that it just ain't so. Not even our Chief Executive Economist can create full employment all the time by signing here and signing there. If he could, what's he waiting for?

The airlines aren't sure they'll buy SST's right away, but they know the fast birds will yield them pure profits if used sometime in the future. And they wouldn't mind a few being developed at public expense. It's like asking a group of speed freaks if they think it would be a good idea if *you* took a trip to T.J. to get some crystal.

A Nixon bootlicker out of Lockheed indicated we should build the SST because it will help to get us all closer together, promoting international understanding. And that's not all. It will boost the U.S. economy, generating tax dollars to fight all our social ills. If we don't support the SST, the social problems of the future will really bring us down. Maybe the head of Boeing is convinced by that argument, but taxpayers can certainly spot it as pure, unadulterated rotting gray matter. If the White House is so concerned about social problems, then let it take the $2 billion from the SST project and help out those in need *directly*. Why go by way of the already heavily subsidized airline industry?

There are also certain environmental problems associated with the new wonderbird. The din you hear from a 707 is nothing compared to the SST. The bang zone of the SST's sonic boom is about fifty miles. That's only the width. The length is the entire length of supersonic flight—2000 to 3000 miles. It has been calculated that if overland sonic transport is permitted, there'll be a boom in every room for those unlucky 500,000,000 people in the world within the bang zone of all the passing SST's. Colonel Robert Stephens, U.S. Air Force officer and technical assistant for SST development, said people could get used to the boom. "It'd be just like the train passing their homes." Bullshit. Why should 95 percent of us be subjected to ear shattering noises for the benefit of those rich 5 percent who'll fly in the speedy mothers? Airliner passengers are already imposing costs on other people without giving any compensation.

Something is finally being done about all this. After one test landing of the Concord 002 at London's Heathrow Airport, the populace was up in arms. The SST may never be allowed there again.

And the City of Boston filed a $10.2 million suit against nineteen airlines, charging them with noise damage in schools near Logan International Airport. The noise is so bad that teachers must interrupt classes once every six minutes.

Therein lies one solution to airplane noise problems. Airlines could be required to compensate everybody whose property depreciates because it is located near an airport or under a flight pattern. Studies could be made of how much land value depreciated and the owner could be duly compensated. It may be that the price tag will be so high that airlines will prefer to pay for more expensive, quieter planes. Then air fares will increase, but so what? Shouldn't the users of jets be required to pay the full price of their flights, including costs of noise or of noise abatement?

The noise problem isn't the only thing caused by the SST and regular jets. There's an air-pollution problem, too. Opponents of the SST claim it will increase the water vapor content of the stratosphere, leading to climatic changes that could screw up the world. The amount of hydrocarbons released into the air will be staggering.

Exhaust pollution from all kinds of jets is a cost on society not borne by airline users. We should tax planes according to how much economic damage they impose on others. There will then be an incentive to have better, lower-pollution engines. But some people oppose the government's drive to get rid of jet smoke. The Air Line Pilots Association does because pilots use jet smoke as an easy way to spot and steer clear of other planes. Every action seems to have a cost.

In some ways it probably appears stupid to most of you that the airlines want to buy bigger and faster planes. It looks like the faster the planes in the air, the longer the waiting time around the airport. Do you rich executives (if you've read past the first page of this book) rejoice over the hours you spend circling O'Hare? Do all you people living under the stacking pattern like the sweet vibes from jet engines? Do all you deplaners like waiting forty-five minutes for your luggage? In this world of growing shortages, there seems to be too many planes around already. Right? Well, almost. You could also say that there are too few airports, but you still wouldn't be right on the nose. The problem is that airports aren't being used well. Half the time they're empty, the rest of the time they're loaded to the sky—and beyond.

If you look at how airport authorities price the services of an airport, you realize somebody has screwed up. Whether you land a 747 or a Piper Cub, you essentially pay the same price, almost nothing. If you try to land at 4:00 P.M., when there are twenty-five planes stacked up behind you, the fee is the same as the one charged at 2:00 in the morning when there are no planes stacked up. (The pilots and passengers are home with those commuters I already told you about.) Something's got to be wrong.

A 747 costs a lot to operate. It holds lots of people. When it flies around for an extra hour, tons of fuel are burned up and valuable time lost. Why shouldn't the planes in front of the 747 be forced to pay for holding it up? And why shouldn't the 747 be forced to pay for all the planes *it* holds up?

It's been estimated that the cost of an additional jet landing at LaGuardia during the rush hour is about $1000—that includes all the gas and time involved in delaying other landings. Right now, no airline takes this cost to other people into account, because nobody has yet devised a way of making them pay everybody affected. Airports can, though. All they have to do is charge a high price for planes that land during the busy times. Keep raising the rush-hour landing fee until a few airlines and private plane owners decide it's better for them to land at less crowded times or not at all. Since for some reason we have private airlines but not many private commercial airports, the only way you're going to get this scheme into effect is to pester the hell out of your local government. Had we allowed Capitalists to own the airports in the first place, you'd hardly have noticed a "shortage" of facilities. Profit seekers would have raised peak-load landing fees a long time ago, and would have expanded capacity because they would have made more bread that way.

Another way out of our present mess would be to auction off the technically feasible number of landing rights to the highest bidder. The most valuable flight would then land at the most convenient hour. People using jets during that time would probably have to pay a higher price. They'd be preventing other people from landing then, so they should pay for the privilege. The money from the auction could be used to expand airport facilities.

There's another reason airports are so busy during prime hours. The incredibly screwed-up FAA won't let airlines compete on a price basis. One way they do compete is by offering better service. Obviously, service is "better" if a company can offer air travelers prime-time scheduled take-offs and landings. Hence we see four different airlines all leaving Kennedy for the same place at about the same prime time. And these four planes are each only half full. If the government would quit enforcing a monopoly in airline travel and would let companies charge what they want, we'd most likely see them trying to cut costs so as to cut prices. They'd fill up the planes more, fly fewer of them, and cut down on airport crowding. As an added attraction, there'd be less jet engine noise and pollution.

None of these seemingly crazy proposals will be adopted, though, because the FAA is run by the airlines and a few cretin bureaucrats. Therefore, I suggest you bring ample reading matter on all future flights. You might not have to use it, though, for if you're lucky your plane will be hijacked. For some reason, ground control lets those planes land immediately.

15.

THE CASE OF THE MISSING GUANO

In 1965, 170,000 tons of bird droppings were harvested from Peru's Chincha Norte Island. In 1969, only 35,000 tons were harvested. Who stole the guano? The guano company would sure like to know, for it sells the nitrogen-rich excrement for fertilizer. Already over $3 billion worth has been harvested since the mid-nineteenth century.

The guano company suspected that the CIA was hauling the bird droppings away at night, but a thorough surveillance canceled out that possibility.

The reason there's so little bird doodoo on Chincha Norte

Island is because there are fewer and fewer birds around there. And the reason there are fewer birds is because the birds are starving. The reason they're starving is because they simply can't get enough to eat.

Why? Because the main source of their diet, anchovies, is being hunted for fishmeal. In 1968 Peru netted 10 million tons of those salty little creatures. The anchovy catch has increased over 4000 percent in little more than a decade. Fewer anchovies in the water means fewer cormorants. Fewer cormorants means fewer bird droppings and less fertilizer for Peru.

But biologists also point out that fewer cormorants will eventually mean fewer anchovies. For the bird droppings sometimes hit the sea. This fertilizes the plankton, which is the main source of food for anchovies.

Wow, what a mess. Look at it!

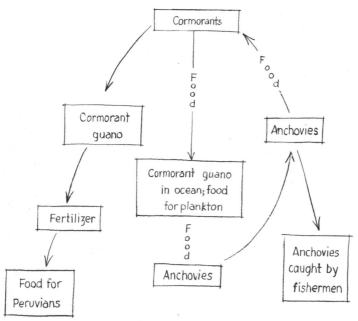

How are we ever going to solve the guano-anchovy problem?
Everything affects everything else.

Imagine a different situation. Let's say that one Pig Capitalist owned the guano fields, the oceans with the anchovies,
and also all the birds. Would he let the cormorants die off?
Would he let the anchovies be overfished? Probably not.
One thing is certain, though, the Capitalist will extract every
last peso he can out of the stuff he's invested in. He'll look
at the value of the bird excrement; at the value of the
anchovies; and also at the biological relation between the
birds, their droppings, and the fish. You can be sure that
he'd harvest just the right amount of anchovies so that just
the right amount of birds live and crap on the island and
into the sea. (By so doing he'd really get his shit together.)
And he doesn't just look at the profits today; he tries to
get the most money forever and ever, greedy bastard that
he is. You'd do the same if given the chance. He therefore
won't want to wipe out the anchovy schools just because
he could make a wad this year, because that would probably
mean less in overall profits.

But no one Pig Capitalist owns the whole mess. There are
lots of fishermen; and also there's the guano company. The
fishermen impose costs on the guano harvesters because
they take away the food for the feces-producing birds. The
birds bestow benefits on the fishermen. The birds also eat
anchovies, so that's a cost to the fishermen. The trouble
arises because all these costs and benefits are not paid for
or perhaps not even considered by the parties they do not
affect directly. The birds certainly are not worried about
how eating anchovies hurts the pescadores. Economists call
this a type of externality problem. It's really just a problem
in contract enforcement though. The guano company and
the fishermen could conceivably get together and work out
a contractual arrangement such that the benefit from an-

chovies and bird guano was greatest. If the contract were enforced, society would be better off, because it would be getting the most out of available resources and that is not *mierda,* or is it?

It's hard to get all the fishermen together to agree not to cheat on any contract. But since the state controls the men, it could enforce any deal made with the guano company (which it also owns).

I'm sure that Peru will sooner or later realize what it has to do. Then we'll see the optimum quantity of shit.

16.

SMOKE ME, I CAN BE HAZARDOUS

Cigarettes aren't hazardous, they're murder. Smoke them all your life and you're almost assured of an early grave. While you're leading up to it you'll feel bad, off and on, and really lousy the rest of the time. Man, like if cyclamates are banned because a few rats dropped dead, why are cigarettes still around?

The rat stage was passed long ago. Tars and nicotines gave

the furry little bastards lung cancer. A few studies were released to the public then, but not much was done.

Then the evidence in humans began piling up. Studies first showed a distinct correlation between smoking and cancer. We all know that correlation doesn't necessarily imply causality. Cancer could cause smoking. Better, more-controlled studies have been done now and few doubts remain: The effect is lung cancer; the cause is smoking. The American Tobacco Institute certainly doesn't agree, but do you expect those profiteering sob's to sell their profits down the drain?

Tobacco also is addictive, certainly as much as grass, so why not be consistent and outlaw both?

Research has proven that cigarette smoking alters the body's chemistry and therefore must be classified as physically addictive. Scientists found this out during an investigation. They wanted to see why *ex*-smokers gained so much weight after quitting the wickedest of weeds. (Funny, smoking good weed does just the opposite.) It turned out that smoking increases metabolism because it causes the thyroid glands to work harder; therefore kicking the habit slows down metabolism and results in weight gain even with the same diet as before. Scientists also found that nicotine increases the body's output of norepinephrine, a nerve stimulant which probably accounts for faster heartbeat in smokers.

Apparently enough Congressmen were convinced about the evils of tobacco to pass legislation, and cigarette ads have been banned from the airways since January 1971. *The New York Times* has taken up the battle and is refusing tobacco ads, while *The New Yorker* and that bastion of learning, the *Readers Digest,* have long rejected cigarette advertising.

While all these people are looking out for the public interest, the cats in HEW are also doing their bit. Someone has estimated that several millions in government funds are being poured into research on smoking and cancer, and also on information dissemination to the public.

It may shock you to find out that at the same time our astute government is also spending enormous amounts for the benefit of tobacco farmers. We've got government research stations finding out the best way to grow the foul weed, and the best way to protect it from its natural enemies. If that's not enough, the government made sure that tobacco growers got monopoly profits by effectively restricting the amount of acreage planted. Anybody who got a license to grow tobacco was treated to a free gift of about $2000 an acre. Today it's been estimated that we give away $80 million a year in tobacco subsidies.

Maybe you should ask your Senator to explain what's happening. First you'd better make sure he doesn't own some tobacco land himself.

If smoking causes cancer, and everyone knows it, why do millions continue fouling up their lungs? *That* many people can't be stupid. The explanation is actually quite simple. Smoking Winstons gives you pleasure now, if that's your trip. You won't feel the fatal effects until many years hence. If you're really into nicotine, your present pleasure far outweighs the cost of losing a few years on the other end of your life. Why not smoke? To be sure, if you knew you'd drop dead tomorrow your decision would be not to smoke, unless you were suicidal. But you obviously don't value a few years of more living, say, thirty years from now as much as you do an extra year starting tomorrow. The further into the future the cost (or pleasure) of any action, the less you value it. The closer any cost (or pleasure) that is incurred, the more you value it. Simple hedonistic calculations.

Since most smokers are now quite well aware of the consequences of their actions, I shouldn't tell them they can't go ahead with smoking if the pleasure principle drives them to continue. It's good dirty oral fun. I'm not God, nor you either. It turns out that government interdictions against nicotine is a waste of time and taxpayers' money.

Make smoking illegal, and we'll have another Prohibition on our hands. The only group who'll gain from that, besides a few Mormons, is the Mafia.

17.

NADER TO THE RESCUE

All you frightened consumers out there must be high on happiness because you now have a friend or two in Washington. The age of consumerism is upon us. It all started with a brilliant lawyer named Ralph Nader who took one ride in a Corvair and ended up with *Unsafe at Any Speed*. Since taking on the GM giant single-handedly, Mr. Nader has tackled the ICC, the FDA, bad air, bad water, bad products, and bad vibes.

Realizing the name of the game, our political machine assigned consumer aides to Congress and the President. And in 1969 there were more than 150 consumer-oriented bills introduced on the floors of the Capitol Building. States have also seen the light. New York City has a Department of Consumer Affairs started by Mayor Lindsay.

Nader and Co. have your best interests at heart. The amount of government waste, inefficiency, and downright detrimental action uncovered by Nader must have been surprising to you all. For this kind of relentless uncovering of federal worthlessness we must salute our bright young lawyer. But let's see what R. Nader has suggested we do about all the unsafe cars, poisonous foods, foul air, and phony advertising.

Take the regulation of interstate commerce. Nader's research fully revealed how the only people benefiting from ICC were the shippers, not the consumers. The ICC has been running a tightly knit cartel for the past eighty-five years, gently screwing the public in the process.

Now, Nader wants to abolish the ICC along with the CAB and the Federal Maritime Commission. But he doesn't leave off there. He wants to put all three together into one gigantic single octopus agency. The agency would supposedly rely more on competition than on regulation.

But I ask you: How long would that last? People serving on regulatory agencies like the easy life. Soon a cozy little arrangement among the superagency and all interstate shippers would develop. We'd be right back where we started from. How can such a bright lawyer ignore such an obvious point?

But who will protect us from the greed of the shippers? Just that. Their greed coupled with your greed. How do railroads make bread? By getting people to buy tickets and by sending freight on trains. How do trucks make profits? Only by getting lots of business. All forms of transportation are in competition with each other. And since you don't like to pay more than you have to for things you buy and trips you take, you reward low-cost shippers and passenger carriers by giving them more business. You don't need protection from the railroads, moving companies, and airlines. You need protection from the federal tentacles taking hold of everything. Don't let the Chief Raider suck you into thinking that the solution to government screwups is a merger of agencies.

What about the millions of Americans who are injured each year in their own homes because of hazardous consumer products? Product-related injuries are costing us $5.5 billion a year. As the President's Commission on Product Safety put it: "The exposure of consumers to unreasonable product hazards is excessive by any standard of measurement." The *Report* of the Commission went on to indicate that "many hazards . . . are unnecessary and can be eliminated without substantially affecting the price to the consumer."

So the truth is finally out. Piggies are making products which could be made safer at *no extra cost*. You knew it all along, right? But does that make much sense? If you really wanted safer products and Capitalists could make them at no extra cost, wouldn't there be an incentive for some of them to get more of you as customers? Wouldn't competition among the greedy Pigs eventually force all of them to make safer products, if that's what you wanted and it didn't cost them anything?

Where's the hang up? Obviously, it *does* cost more to make safer products. Nothing's free anymore (and never was).

You are the ones responsible for hazardous products because you don't want to pay for 100 percent safety all the time. You'd rather buy products which have a small probability of causing injury but which cost less than those with a near zero probability of being hazardous.

I'm full of it. You really do only want the safest things money can buy, you say. Apparently not enough of you feel that way because otherwise profiteering manufacturers would be making bread by catering to your extreme desire never to get hurt.

Sure, some of you get maimed or killed by faulty products, but does that mean *all* of us should go without relatively low-priced goods so that *all* accidents can be eliminated? You've already made the choice. Are you going to be pushed around by people like Nader and a president's commission?

The Commission recommended that "Broad responsibility for the safety of consumer products should be vested in a conspicuously independent Federal regulatory agency, a Consumer Product Safety Commission."

What did you expect? One commission breeds another. The history of regulation in America has been one of public waste and support of private monopolies, all to the detriment of the general public. No thanks. We need a product safety agency like we need a third anus.

The President's Commission also stated that a Consumer Safety Advocate would be around to let the voice of the consumer be heard. You like the idea? You've already got a President's Special Assistant for Consumer Affairs. She's done a lot for you, and she's proud of it. In her purse she carries a little note hand-scratched by Nixon himself. It says: "I'm with you all the way because I'm on a low fat diet myself." Dick was referring to all the hard work your Consumer Affairs lady put into preventing hot dog Capitalists from increasing the fat content of weenies. Now I ask you, do you want the quality and price of your hot dogs determined by a fat jowled man and his weight-watcher assistant? Well, that's what you're getting now. It will only grow worse if you let the government step in with more regulation, more agencies, and more benevolent special assistants to look out for your well-being.

Don't stop now, Mr. Nader. Keep uncovering all the bad things in our society. But that's it. We can take care of ourselves. We thank you for all the information you're providing. But no more regulations, please.

DUDES--HAVE A CUP OR TWO,
BUT THEN DON'T SCREW

You may not believe it, but coffee
should be banned. The scientific evidence is already over-
whelming. Caffein injected into pregnant female rabbits
caused embryonic death or greatly retarded development
in their offspring. Caffein caused mutations in sea urchins,
in plants, in bacteria, in fungus, in fruitflies, and in little
furry mice.

One biochemist working for the Food and Drug Administration found that caffein screws up human lung cells *in vitro*. Though most of us don't walk around wearing test tubes over our lungs, it's still a scary idea.

In 1963 a study of 2000 middle-aged middle-class men found a high correlation between coffee drinking and heart disease. (Query: Does heart disease cause coffee drinking?) Since coffee drinking causes a rise in the level of fatty acids and serum lipids (fat in the blood), and some of those things are known to cause coronary heart disease, is there little wonder about this fact?

Well, are you convinced? Not yet? I have another little-known fact. Men suffer chromosomal damage by drinking "essence of old shoes." [1] Chicks don't have to worry about it, since all their DNA replication of germinal cells ceases at birth (their own, that is). Do you realize the implications of this? Cats are making new spermies every day. If coffee drinking splits apart these newly forming chromosomes, then a lot of mutated people can blame (if they are capable) that cup of Folgers. One study found that the "total amount of genetic damage due to caffein [is] in the neighborhood of a natural mutation rate . . . There is the strong likelihood that caffein may prove to be one of the most dangerous mutagens in man."

Could coffee drinking be responsible for the one in fifty babies born with a severe malformation in the U.S.? Enough dudes guzzle the stuff. Americans drink more coffee than milk. About four out of five adults drink coffee every day and almost a quarter of these drinkers put away five or more cups a day, day in day out, 366 days a year. Coffee isn't the only means of getting your chromosomes split up. Have a

[1] Ben Jonson.

Coke or Pepsi; or take Excedrin, Dristan, or Anacin. And if you still can't get enough, pop a few No Dōz.

But, like, if there's so much evidence about the bad effects of coffee, then why no info out of the keepers of our Health, Education and Welfare? Maybe we should see how much bread the Pan American Coffee Bureau has been blowing on trips to D.C. lately.

Even if the aromatic picker-upper does such bad things, should we really tick off all those millions of coffee freaks? Outlaw coffee and you end up with Prohibition again. People get what they want anyway, so why support the Mafia by making caffein illegal? (Yuban speakeasies?) The government has the obligation to tell everyone what's wrong with the stuff, but that's all. You may still want to get present pleasure from drinking coffee at the cost of a few more heart attacks later on. Nobody should stop you.

One thing, though, all you coffee-drinking cats should lay off a few days before you ball your old lady, unless, of course, she's on the Pill.

WHAT DO YOU SAY TO
10,000 NAKED LADIES?

Besides wreaking destruction on all the things we must give our body in order to survive, Pig Capitalists are also attempting to destroy our minds. It's getting so everywhere you turn there's a delectable piece staring you in the face. Our nation is being swamped with pornography. Remember the good old days when the dirtiest mags around were the ones that showed a little bare bosom? Now even *Playboy* shows hair and the corner movie house plays full color 3-D movies of every sexual maneuver conceivable and even some which are downright impossible.

Our courts have been getting laxer and laxer in their jobs as guardians of public morality. The Pinko Warren Court was the worst. Some people are distressed, including our favorite heavy thinker Barry Goldwater. He admits that there's some problem in defining what is or isn't obscene. But, says our wise man, "As a father and a grandfather, I know, by golly, what is obscene and what isn't." (Women's Lib, where are you?) Fortunately we've now got a real pre-server of freedom in the Justice Department. You don't have to ask Attorney General John Mitchell twice about his knowledge of pornography. He knows that everything with a hint of hair is bad for society. His fearless mind savers are relentlessly continuing their fight against smut peddlers. Thank God and his partner, Spiro Agnew, a true man after Nixon's heart.

Let's see what's going to happen when the team of Gold-water-Agnew-Mitchell (GAM for short) wins the battle against sexual mind destruction. Let's say that GAM succeeds in getting an amendment to the U.S. Constitution passed which prohibits the manufacture, sale, or transportation of pornographic material within, or the import into, or the export from the United States for excitation purposes. And suppose that to help enforce this amendment GAM gets a Noread Act passed which forbids the purchase, possession, and use of pornographic materials. GAM would then have us going and coming.

Right away, no more legal kicks. Grove Press out of business. *Playboy* banned. *Avant Garde* flushed down the toilet. So, no more smut.

Ho, ho, as the nasty little man with a jello belly once said.

All the legal smut will now be replaced by a close substitute, illegal smut. Man, like some dudes thrive on the stuff. The peddlers will merely go underground. The Mafia will move in. More dirty pictures will be taken in Canada and sneaked across the border—an increase in our imports.[1] The cost of smut peddlers putting out pornography will rise. Why? Well, they can't inform potential customers as cheaply as they could before the GAM amendment. No ads, no book reviews. Also, they've got to pay off the Mafia and the Pigs for not arresting them. And a totally new cost has arisen— the risk of fines and jail. You can be sure that there will be fewer producers of porno books and flicks around.

How about all the horny sex maniacs and frustrated husbands who read to get a little fantastical titillation once in a while? A lot of them might be satisfied with just thinking about it. They might not buy any more smut. Others will need it so badly they'll pay the higher price involved; that is, more expensive salacity and the risk of fines or imprisonment. They'll also have a harder time finding out where to buy high-quality smut that best suits their particular bent (so to speak). Information is not cheap when the peddlers are prevented from advertising and the Feds might have undercover agents posted all over the place. GAM would be really doing all of us a big favor by passing that antismut amendment and the Noread Act—the Mafia would have a new arena of adventure; smut wholesalers would have to pay more to purchase obscene materials; and porno preverts would have to pay more for lower quality excitation.

Well, you might say, at least we'd have fewer sex crimes. But is that for sure? Hardly. The Commission on Obscenity and Pornography concluded that, if anything, pornography

[1] A worsening in our balance of payments.

prevents sex crimes by allowing frustrated Toms, Dicks & Harrys an outlet. It recommended the repeal of all pornographic laws for consenting adults. Though not everyone on the Commission agreed. The Reverend Winfrey C. Link didn't want to see an open sewer run through the minds of America. And a Nixon stooge named Keating was so against the Commission's final report that he fought for an injunction to prevent its publication. Another gentleman has asked Congress to investigate the Committee. And yet another member, who happened to be head of the "Morality in Media" group, was really pissed off. He feared that the U.S. would become another Denmark.

Well, so what? Sex crimes are almost nonexistent in that country. In 1967, when the ban on written porno was lifted, sex crimes dropped 25 percent in Denmark. In 1968 there was another 10 percent decrease. And '69 saw a startling 31 percent drop. And what's more, after all forms of censorship were lifted, sales of pornography to the Danes soon fell. It's not hard to figure out why. Most dudes aren't too turned on by gaping full-color frontal shots.

20.

PASSENGERS WILL PLEASE REFRAIN
FROM FLUSHING TOILET WHILE THE TRAIN IS
IN THE STATION DARLING I LOVE YOU

Ever taken a train? What happened when the call of nature led you to the throne? The usual? Not quite. Didn't you notice that if you looked down at the after mass as it swirled away (don't you always?) the tie crossings below became visible? Well, they should be visible, for the remains of your breakfast were passed right down to them. Free enterprise is allowed to defecate all over the landscape.

A small problem? I'll let you decide. There are more than 30,000 locomotives and 16,000 cabooses in the U.S. That's at least 46,000 johns riding the rails. Since the engineer and his crew have biological needs just like other beings, they use these crappers to their best advantage—52,000,000 pounds of railroad worker excrement a year hit the ground below. Add a little urine here and there and you get (if you're fast) over 32,000,000 gallons of human waste in one form or another added to our natural wonders.

I haven't even counted the passengers, though an ever-diminishing number they may be. That adds another 200,-000,000 pounds of solids. Mix in some passenger water for a grand total of another 90,000,000 gallons of untreated human waste sprucing up the railway landscape.

Why do we let the railroads get away with all this manshit? Buses can't do it. Planes can't do it. So why let the choochoos do it? (Excuse me, Mr. J. Rubin, for the unintended plagiarism.) The railroads maintain that the tracks are their private property. In some sense they're right and we really shouldn't give a shit (so to speak) if the problems of smell and the rest were confined only to the railroad company. Even if the stink is so bad as to offend train passengers, that's no problem, because nobody's being forced to take a train. Since trains are competing against buses, planes, cars, motorcycles, bicycles, and feet, people will take their transportation business elsewhere, if the railway smells offend them.

But there are other problems. Like feces can contain almost thirty communicable diseases. The railroad tracks aren't always fenced off from wandering canines and venturesome kids. Since the tracks are so accessible to children and dogs, we find that railroads can be the cause of spreading disease to unwary families. And since it's impossible to determine where a disease is picked up from, nobody can sue the R.R. for the external bad effects of sewage on tracks if one of their kids comes down with typhoid. Therefore I say that cans that hold the crap should be forced on the railroads. That will mean higher costs and hence higher prices for railway transportation. Shouldn't users of the railroads pay the full cost?

Yeah, and what about those poor workers who gotta put in their days on the excrementally infected tracks making repairs? In some sense, that's already taken care of. Some workers don't like to work in smelly places where they can catch diseases. The railroad has to pay higher wages because it doesn't spend the money on better train johns. The workers obviously make the decision to work on the tracks if the pay is high enough.

That isn't the end of the story though. Workers getting a germ from the tracks don't always have the opportunity to wash after every tie is laid. They come back from a hard day's work and touch stair banisters, door handles, and already filthy lucre which they hand to clerks in payment for the evening's groceries.

Railroad workers spread disease this way. They impose an external cost on others, and those affected have no way of getting compensation from the guilty worker.

The moral of the story—don't ever shake hands with a railroad man.

21.

THE PASSING PIG PARADE

Just look at them, Ameriкккa's finest
—the Pigs. Aren't they sweet, all decked out in steel helmets,
gas masks, riot sticks, and cans of MACE? There was a time
when parents would tell their kids that if they ever got lost,
a policeman would give them an ice-cream cone and help
them. Times they are a-changin'. Many of these same parents now make sure the Pigs never get near their kids. What's
happened? Why have we let America turn into such a police

state that many people are afraid to get within a country mile of a Pig?

The answer is simple. Although those in the know have finally discovered the frightening truth that ghetto dwellers have known for years, there are many Americans around who still think that the Pig Is Man's Best Friend. This same silent majority sees scary things happening. Robbery rates are skyrocketing. Assault rates are skyrocketing. Rapes are the thing of the day. Murder continues upward. And riots and bombings are now so common they no longer make headlines. White America is scared, so the storm troopers of the power structure are called on in full force and given unlimited power. What was a somewhat limited evil with enormous potentialities has become an unbridled nightmare. But neither the real causes nor the best solutions to the current "crime wave" are easy to agree upon.

One idea has been to buy more Pigs and let them handle the crime increase. Not everyone agrees about that particular solution. That great mind of the century, Mrs. Martha Mitchell, knows that "the academic society is responsible for all our troubles . . . They are the people that are destroying our country." If that's the case, then we can't stop crime by more police action, we should just wipe out what that other great mind Spiro called "effete intellectuals."

By definition, crime is committed by criminals. Are more trigger-happy Pigs the way to stop crime? Perhaps, but only if they succeed in making potential crime committers fear detection, apprehension, conviction, imprisonment and/or fines. And even then, it's not certain.

Take a horse freak. Think he cares about going to jail? When a cat is physiologically addicted, the usual inverse relation between action and costs of action disappears. In fact, addicts go to jail more and more often without so much as a fight. Society is obviously wasting its money away on police, courts, and prison for real smack heads. We should be spending our tax bread in rehabilitation for these cats, if we're truly interested in preventing their "crime."

We'd also get a better deal for our police-protection dollar if we'd rid ourselves of laws against crimes with no victims. Like who should care about people blowing grass, about females selling their wares, about consenting adults doing anything they can think up, if no one is hurt in the process? In any one year the total budget for crime prevention is a certain fixed number of dollars. Why squander those dollars on getting "criminals" who didn't cause anyone any harm except maybe lady judges in pairs?

And that's not the only area of "crime" the public authorities waste your money on. In 1967 the Secret Service reported that $1.6 million was lost by the public because of counterfeiters. In 1967 about $9 million in Secret Service expenses went to suppressing counterfeiting, a sure case of the cure being worse than the illness. Is that how you want your tax dollars pissed away?

For every Pig on the Funny Money, Grass, and Pussy Patrol there's one less Pig to prevent murder and robberies. When you middle-class straights realize that fact of life, then maybe a cat will be able to blow his smoke in peace, then maybe closet queens will all come out and be what they dream of being.

Another way we'd halt the rise in crime is to stop making real criminals out of small-time punks out for a kick. Do you know what happens to the nineteen-year-old who gets put behind bars for three and a half years because of a joy ride in a stolen car? One parole officer in S.F. remarked: "I've seen men leave San Quentin so burned out by bitterness that they'll never recover. Things happen in there, terrible things, and a man has no redress. He is helpless when it happens, and his helplessness destroys him." You know what he's talking about. The prisoner is led into a cell with cats accused of everything from petty theft to first degree murder. He's beat up the first night, then used as the cell punchboard and fellatio expert until the other inmates are tired of him. If the dude is convicted and sent to a state pen, "everywhere, every minute there is the threat of violence." And since many cons are adept hardened criminals, the neophyte soon learns the tricks of the trade.

So what happens? Within five years after release 70 percent of the ex-cons are locked up again. Every 1000 first-time offenders will one day become involved in more than 3000 additional arrests. I ask you, is that a smart way to spend on law and order? Instead of stopping crime our prison system breeds criminals. A total reevaluation of our penal system is obviously in order. If a Capitalist unloaded his money on such a losing proposition he'd soon find himself on welfare.

Not only does our prison system accomplish just the opposite of what it's supposed to do, so, too, our court system screws things up. The reason for having courts is to try all accused offenders fairly. Instead, we now have a system of random sentencing, hopelessly clogged court calendars, and DA's willing to strike a bargain with anyone up for trial.

The effects of haphazard sentencing were brought out by what happened to a young kid who pleaded guilty, on the advice of his father, for attempting to rob a grocery store.

The judge gave him ten to twenty. After nine years the cat was paroled. He was somewhat pissed off at the raw deal he had gotten. So he ended up killing fifteen men and robbing $300,000 from banks. Thus John Dillinger repayed society for screwing him.

A thing of the past? Nope. A dude in Atlanta embezzled twenty-five thou from a bank—twenty years. At the same time a cat embezzled twenty-one thou from a credit union —three months. What do you think the first guy is going to be when he gets out of prison, if he survives?

The disparity in prison sentences has no rhyme or reason, and furthermore makes numerous convicted offenders want to get back at society for their "raw deals." In New York State forgers on the average get about twenty-two months in the can. In California they get forty-five months, and in Kansas seventy. The average jail term for a narcotic violation is forty-four months in Connecticut and ninety months in Texas.

Racial and class discrimination in sentencing is even more widespread. Detroit's Blacks get jail sentences twice as long as their lily-white cohorts. And guys in work clothes go to jail more often than dudes going before his Royal Hindass in a tie and coat. The moral? Always have a Brooks Brothers original on hand in case you get busted.

What effect does the disparity in sentencing have on the crime rate? Well, think about it. If I could get ten years for robbing a grocery store and also ten years for robbing a bank, why not try for the bank? The point is that if the punishment does not fit the crime, as they say, then offenders will have little incentive to take smaller risks by committing smaller crimes. Therefore we have more serious crimes because of our screwed-up system of justice.

Some say that crime is rising because our society is getting richer and oppression is getting worse. But that's no excuse for setting up a system which flagrantly spends our money in such a way as to increase, not decrease, offenses; which unabashedly discriminates against the Black and the poor; and which convicts people for crimes against no one except some uptight frustrated holier-than-thous who long ago made laws against enjoyment for the hell of it.

If something isn't changed, we will indeed witness revolution for the hell of it, and the Yippies will come marching home.

22.

EPILOGUE

(Please turn page)

Not
even
a
naked
lunch
is
free.